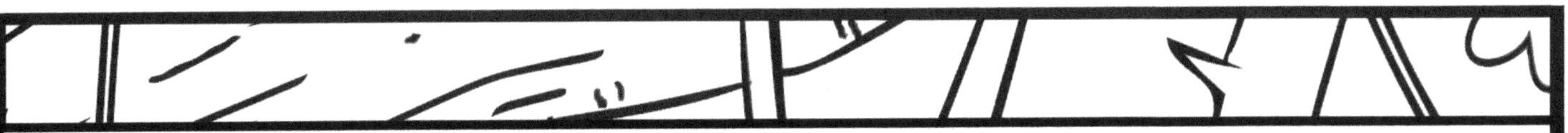

HOW TO DRAW MOBS

THIS BOOK BELONGS TO...

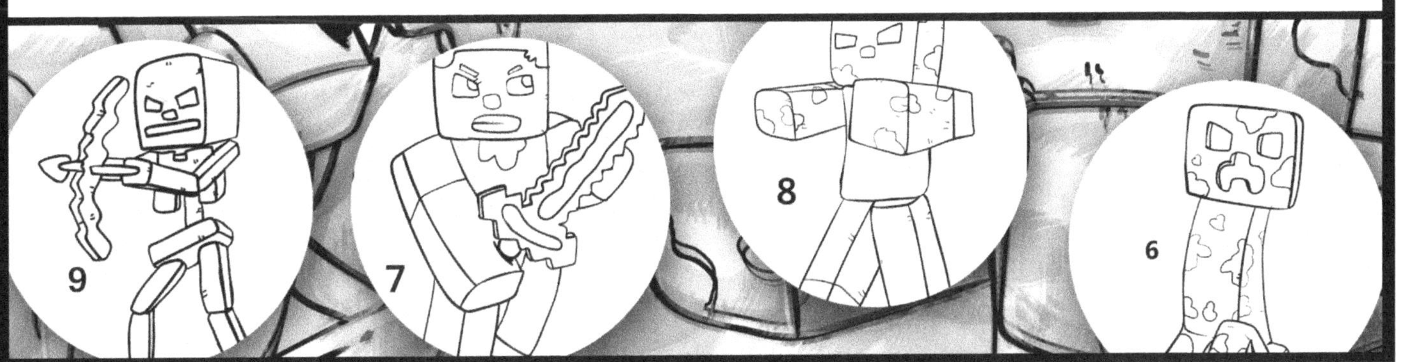

How to Use This Book

Nine Minecraft Scenes

36 Mobs and Items

Hello there! I'm sure you picked up this book because you love Minecraft and you like to draw. Anyone can draw Minecraft stuff, and all you have to do is follow this guide and keep on practicing.

We have featured 36 mobs and items with their detailed step-by-step instructions here. Everything starts as lines and blocks. So, as long as you can draw and copy lines and blocks, you are good to go.

The first few pages will teach you how to draw a Warden, a sculk shrieker, a torch, and Steve, followed by a Minecraft scene that suggests how you can put all of these drawings together.

After working on all the 36 mobs and items and doing the suggested Minecraft scenes, start juicing your creative imagination and creating your own Minecraft scenario.

What are you waiting for? Get those pencils and erasers. Try drawing lightly so that it is easier to erase, and then darken it as you go for your final drawing.

You can do it!

1
2
3
4
5
6
7
8
9
10
11

Now, it's your turn

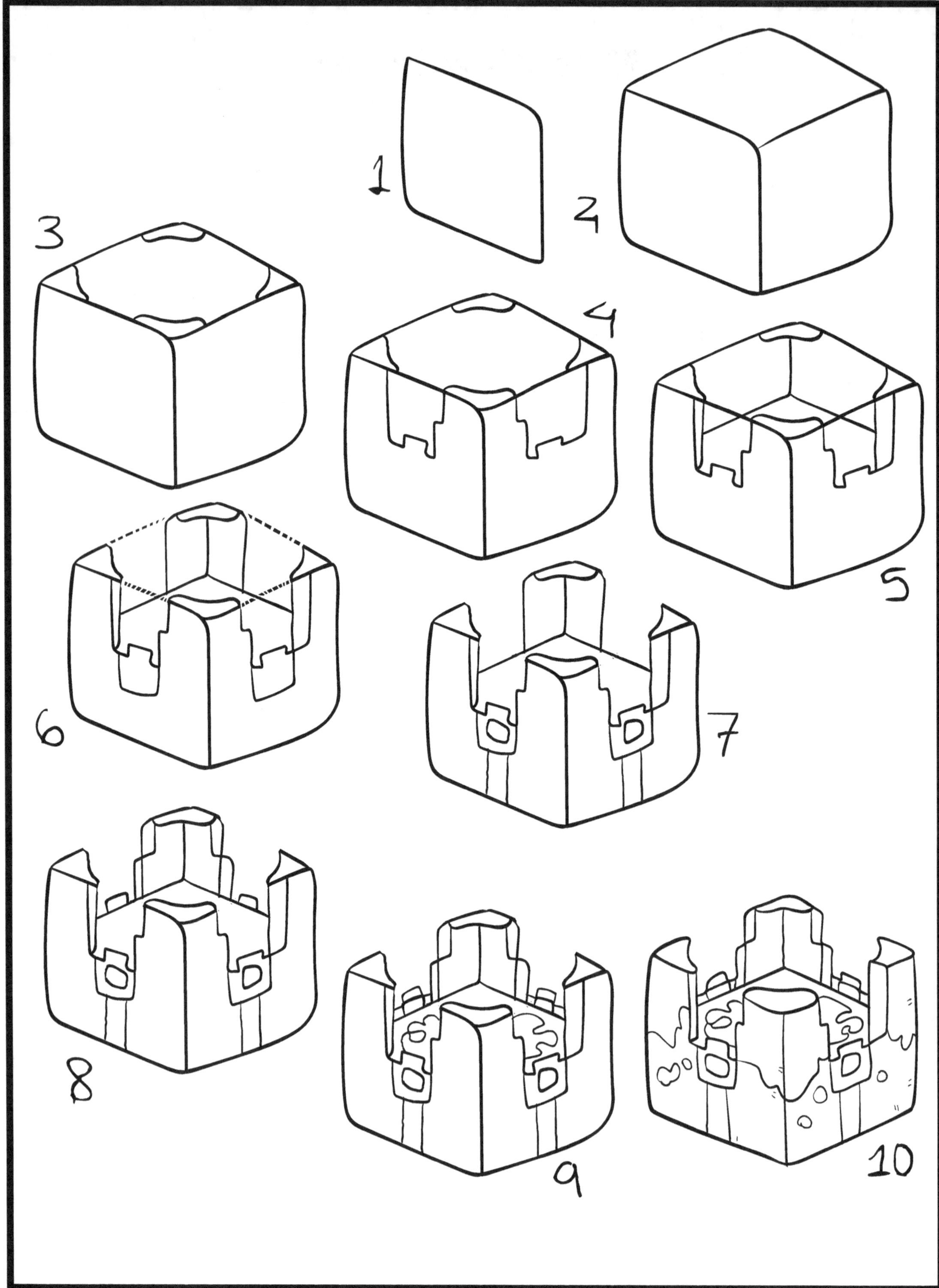

1
2
3
4
5
6
7
8
9
10

Now, it's your turn

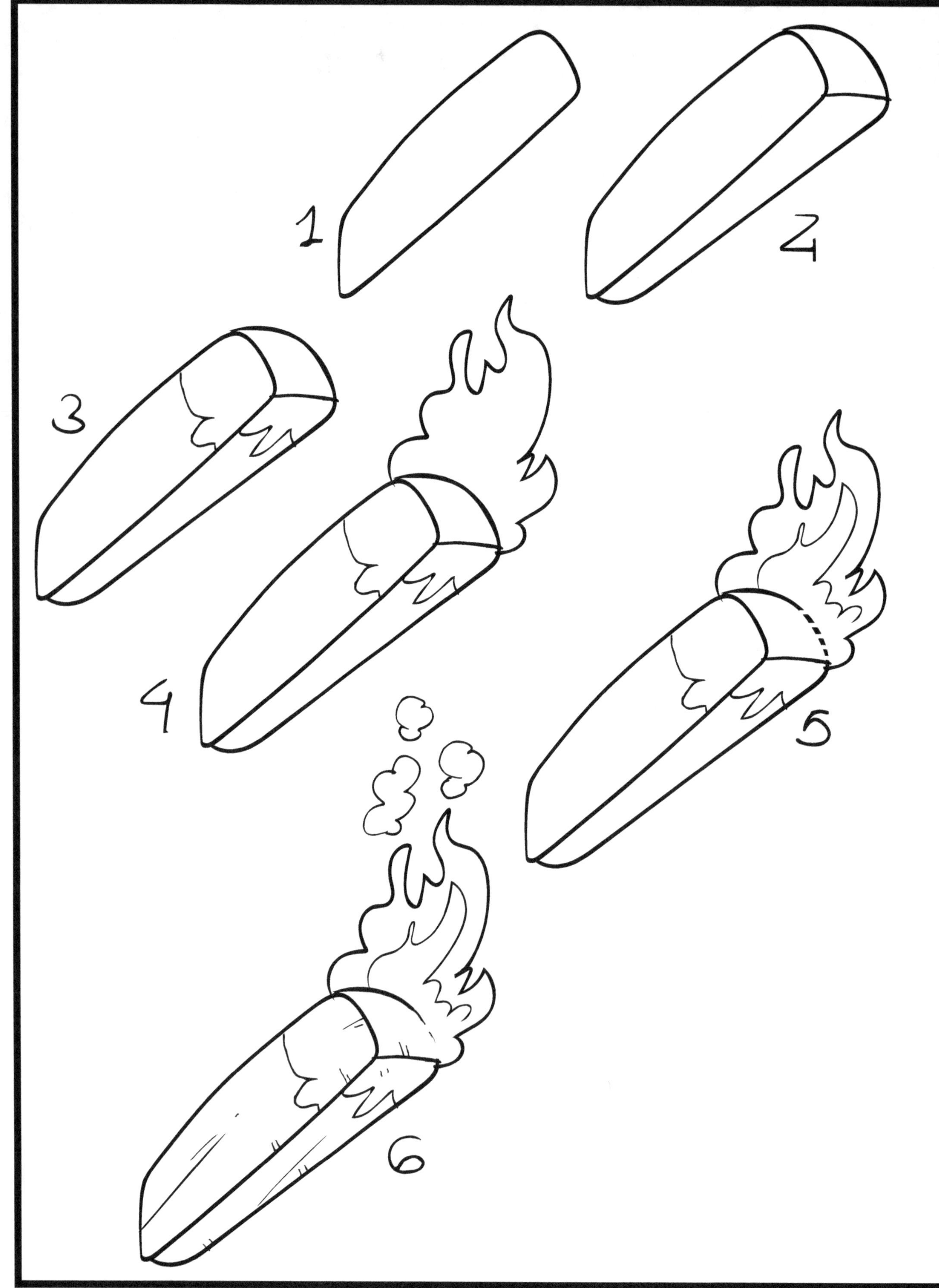

1
2
3
4
5
6

Now, it's your turn

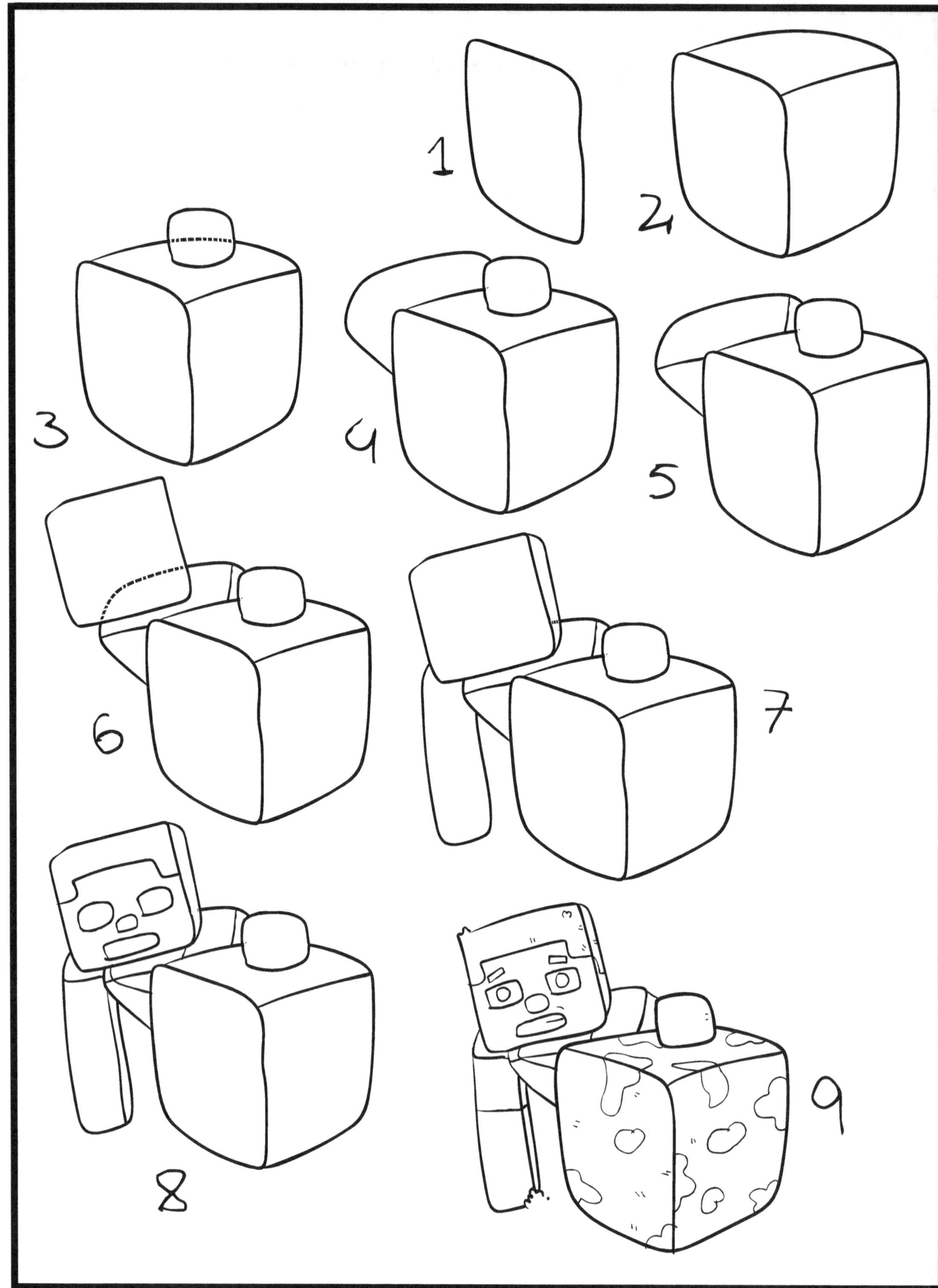

1
2
3
4
5
6
7
8
9

Now, it's your turn

Now, it's your turn

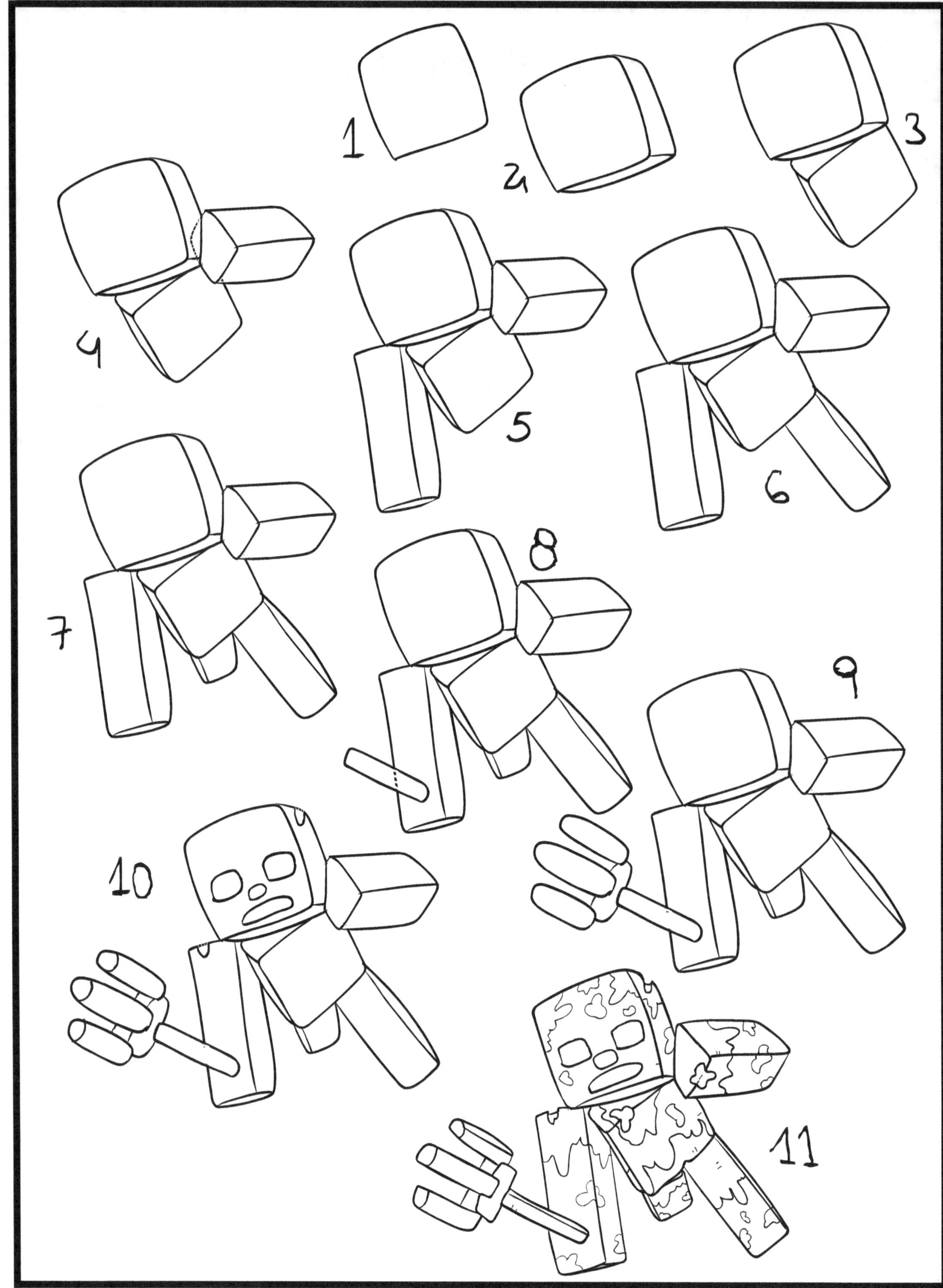

Now, it's your turn

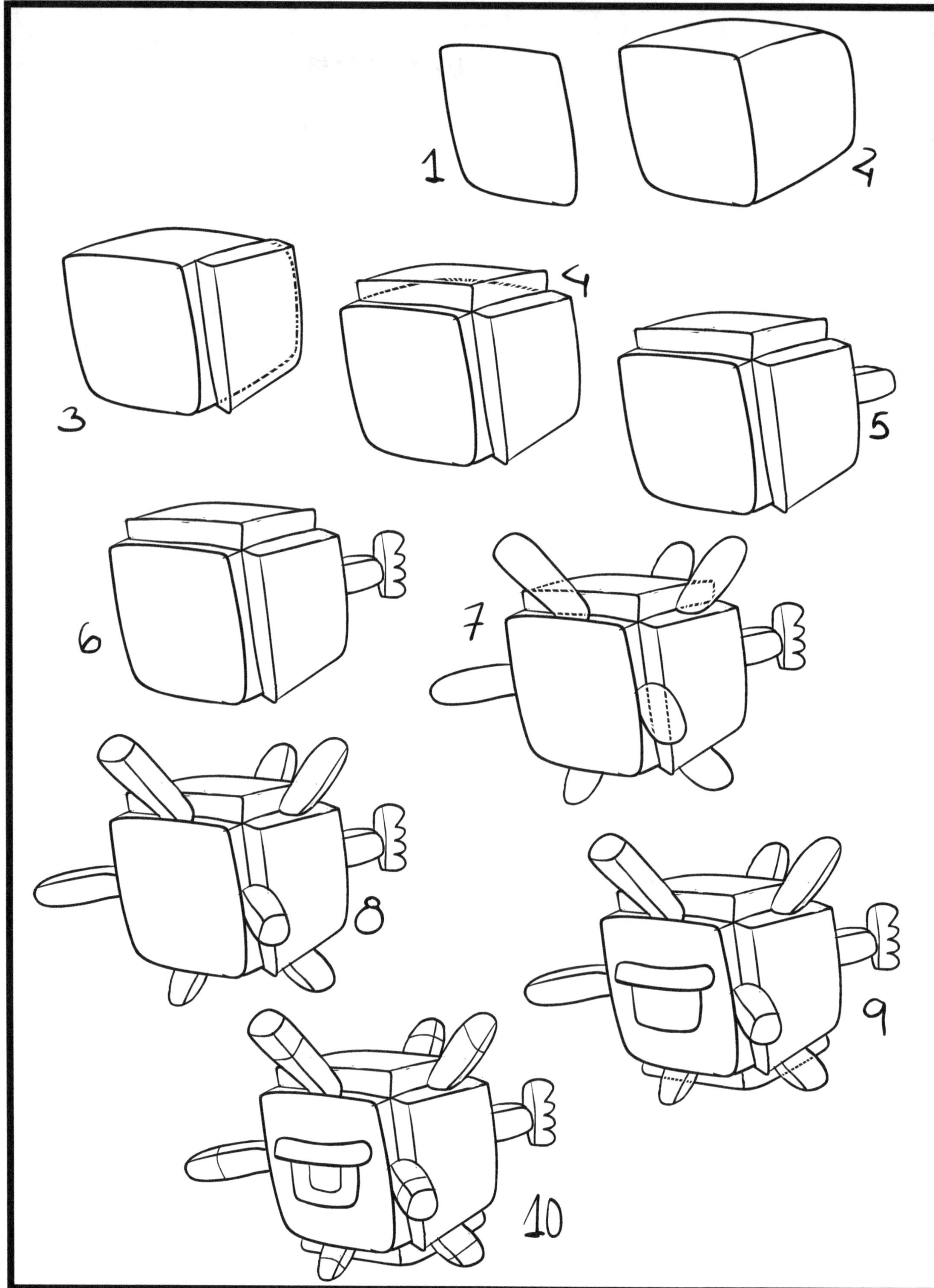

Now, it's your turn

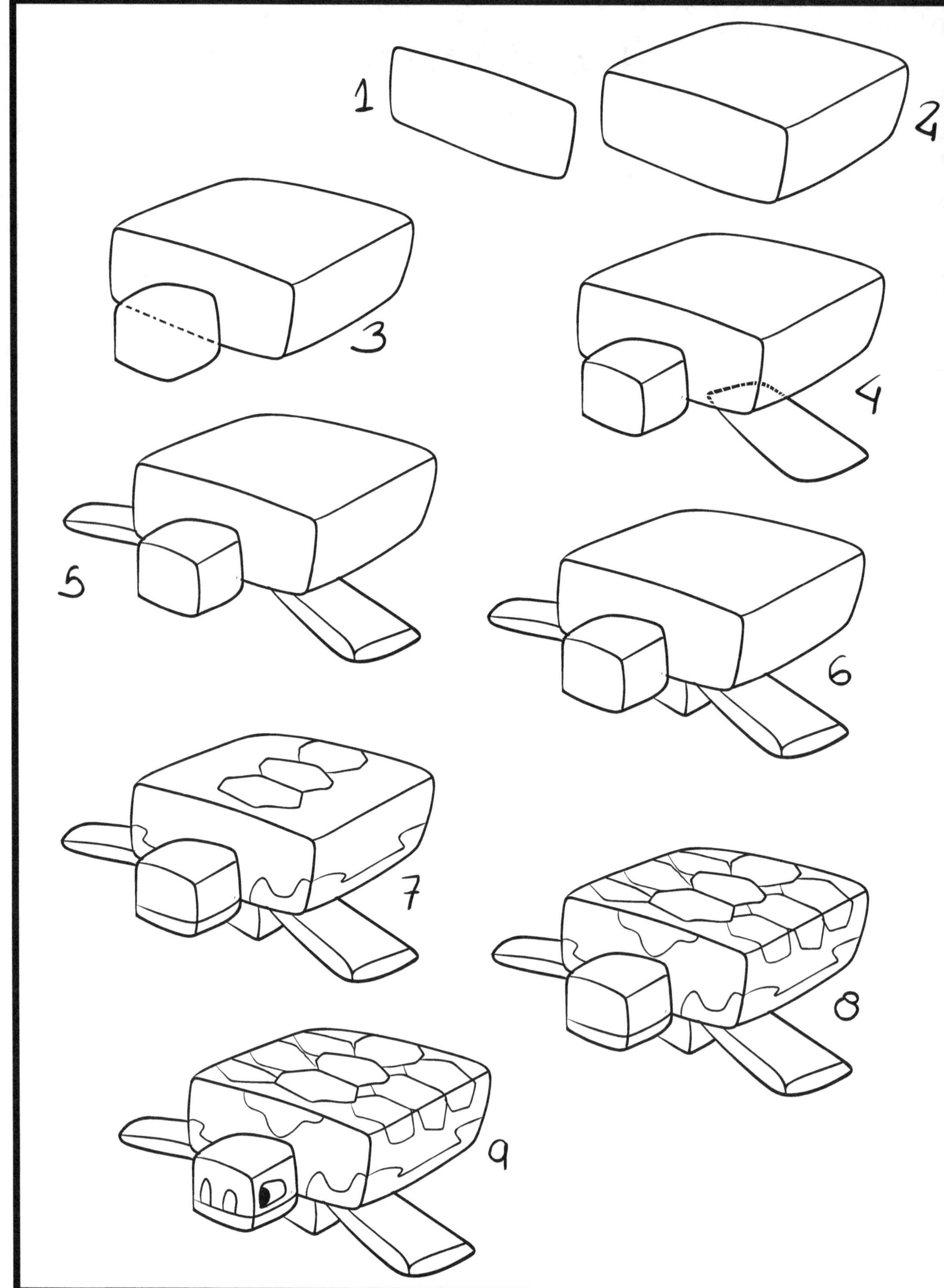

Now, it's your turn

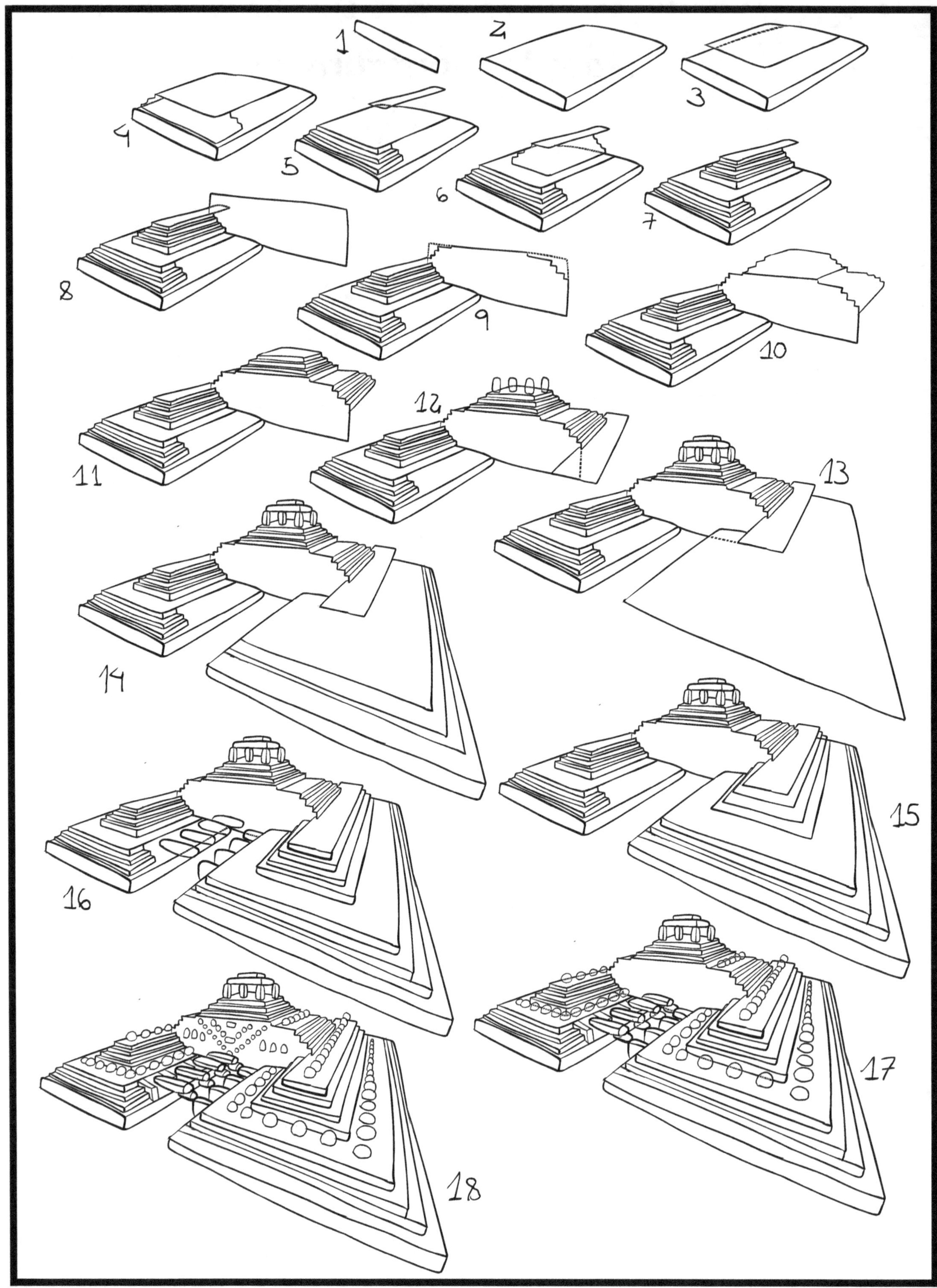

1
2
3
4
5
6
7
8
9
10
11
12
13
14
15
16
17
18

Now, it's your turn

Now, it's your turn

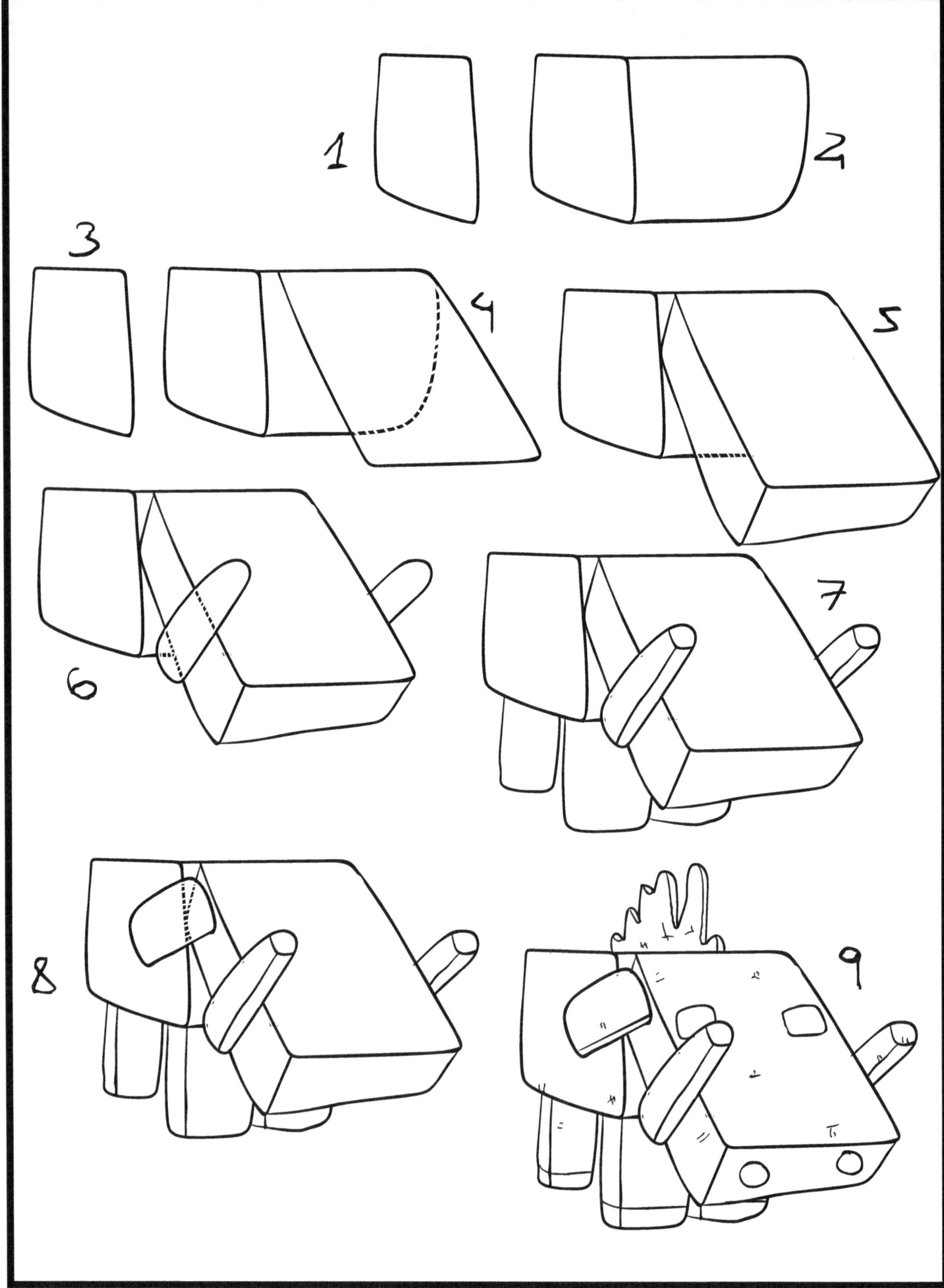

1
2
3
4
5
6
7
8
9

Now, it's your turn

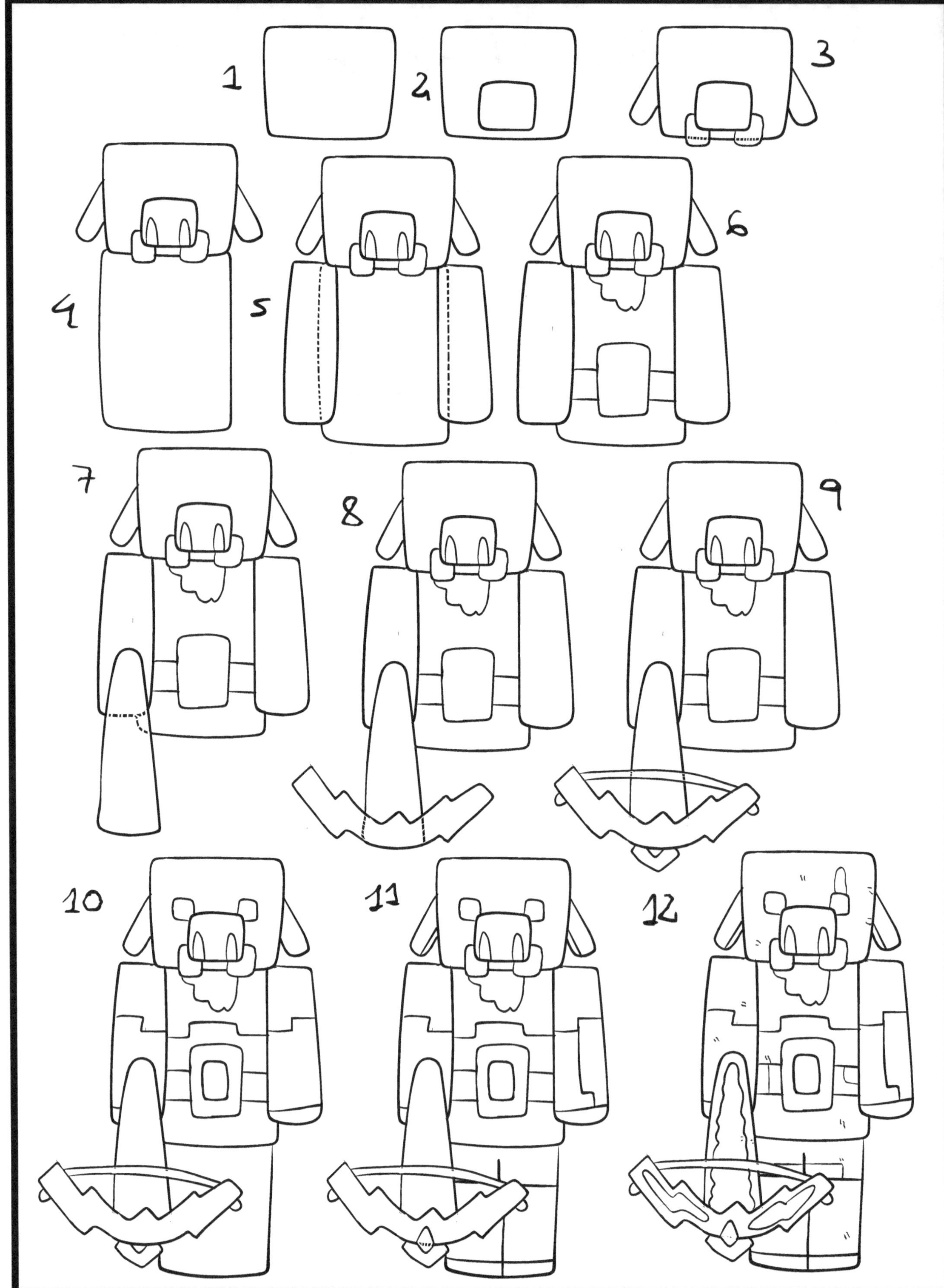

Now, it's your turn

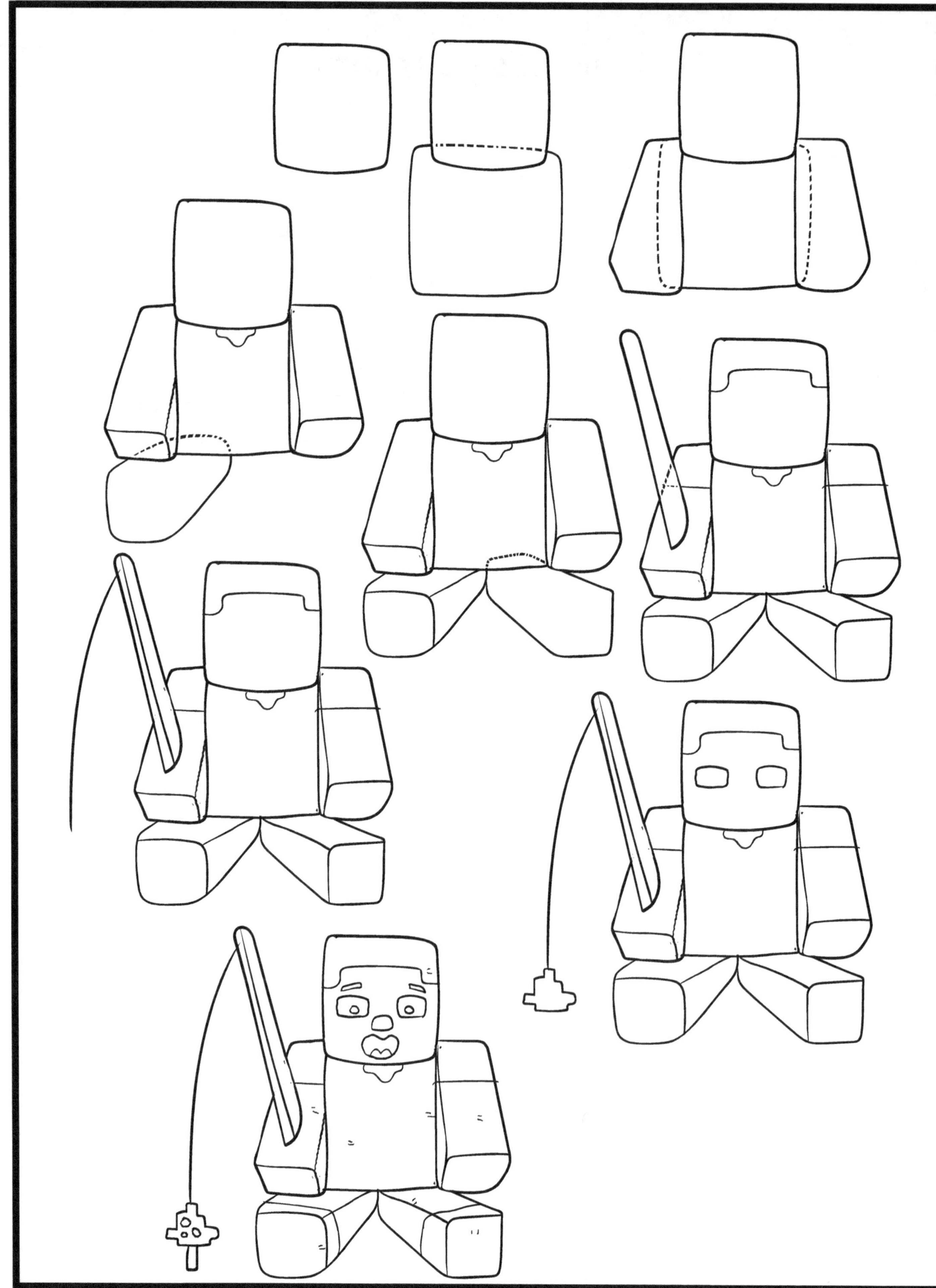

Now, it's your turn

Now, it's your turn

Now, it's your turn

1
2
3
4
5
6
7
8
9
10
11

Now, it's your turn

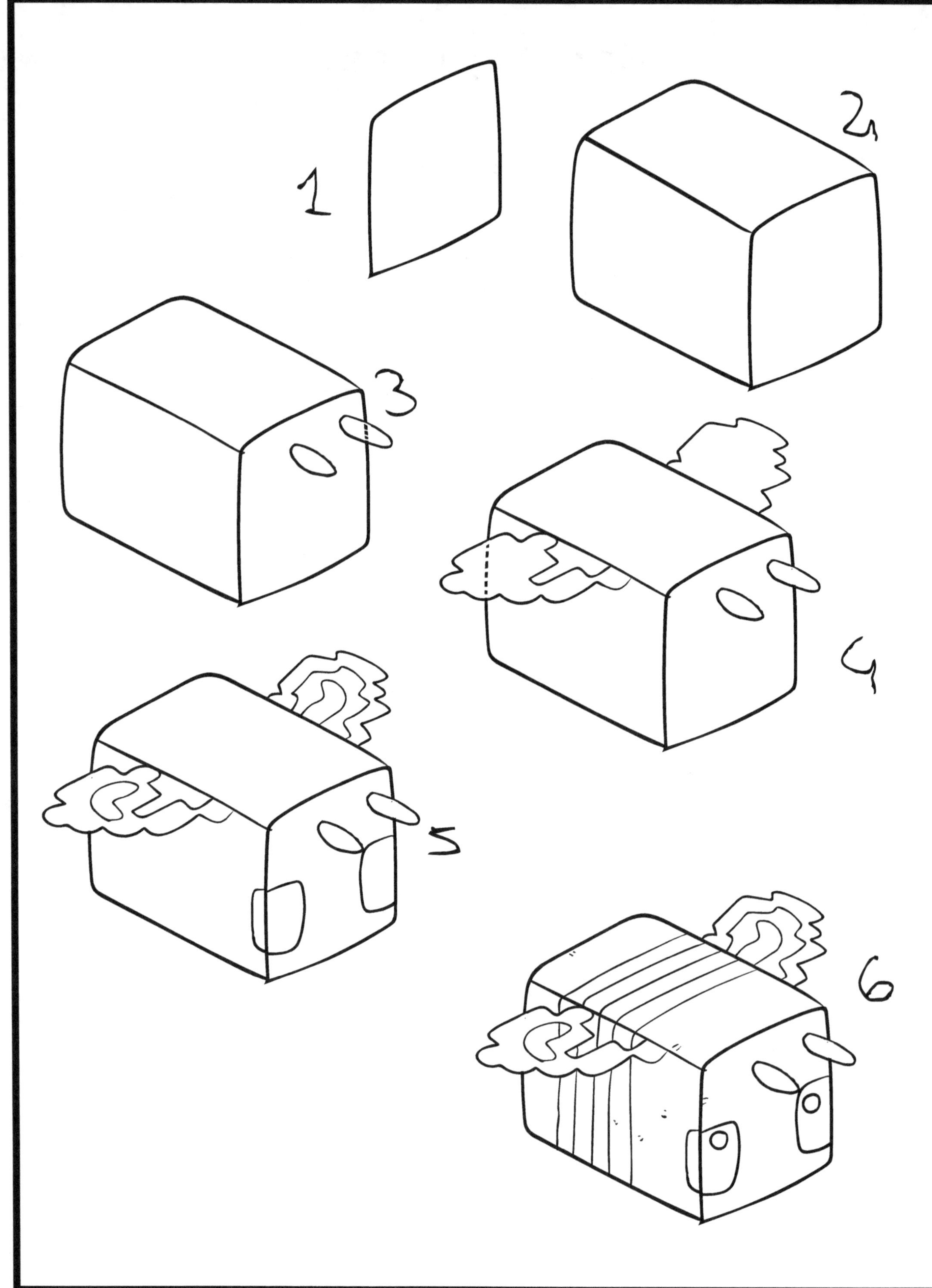

1
2
3
4
5
6

Now, it's your turn

1
2
3
4
5
6
7
8
9
10
11
12

Now, it's your turn

Now, it's your turn

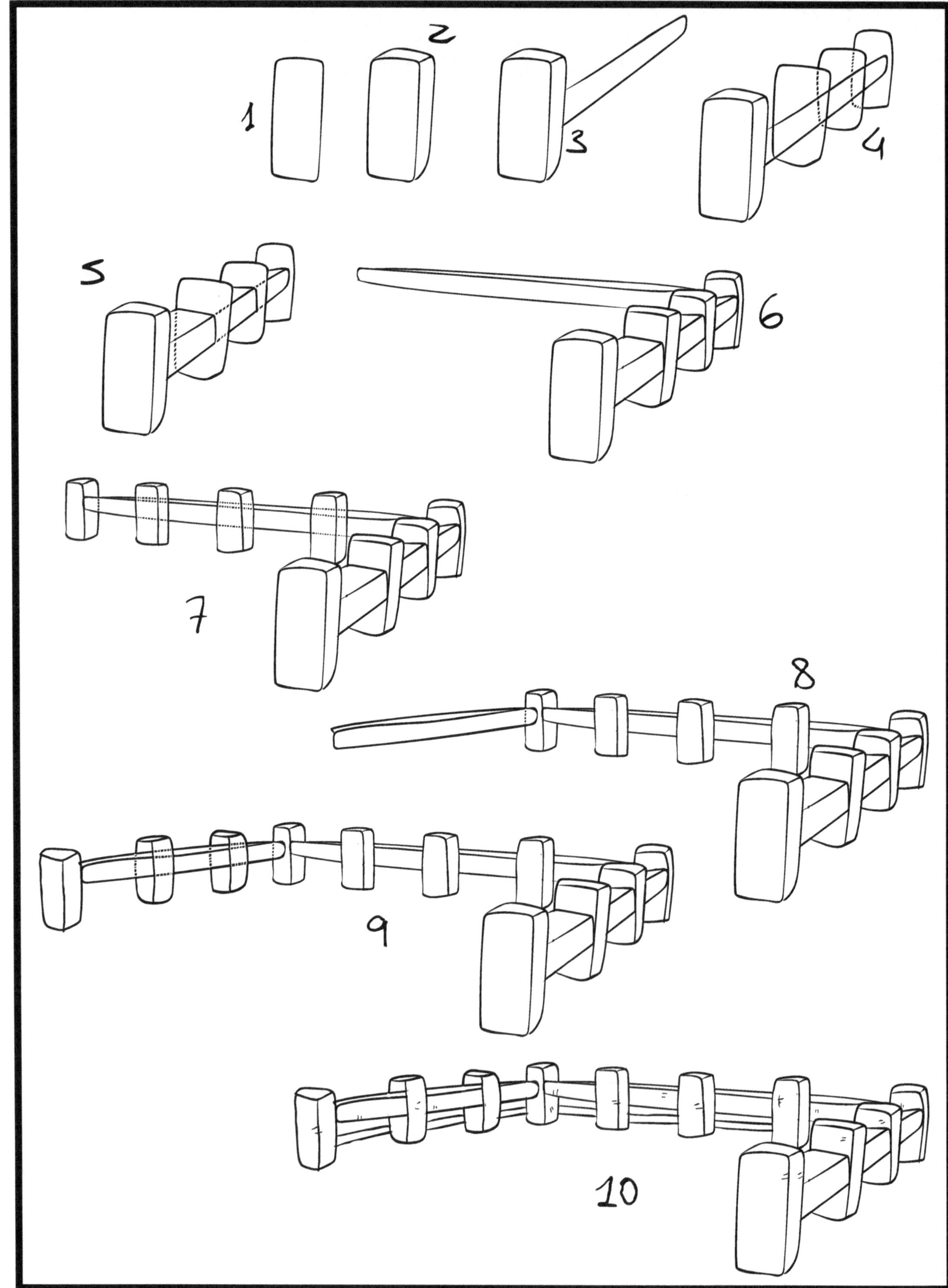

Now, it's your turn

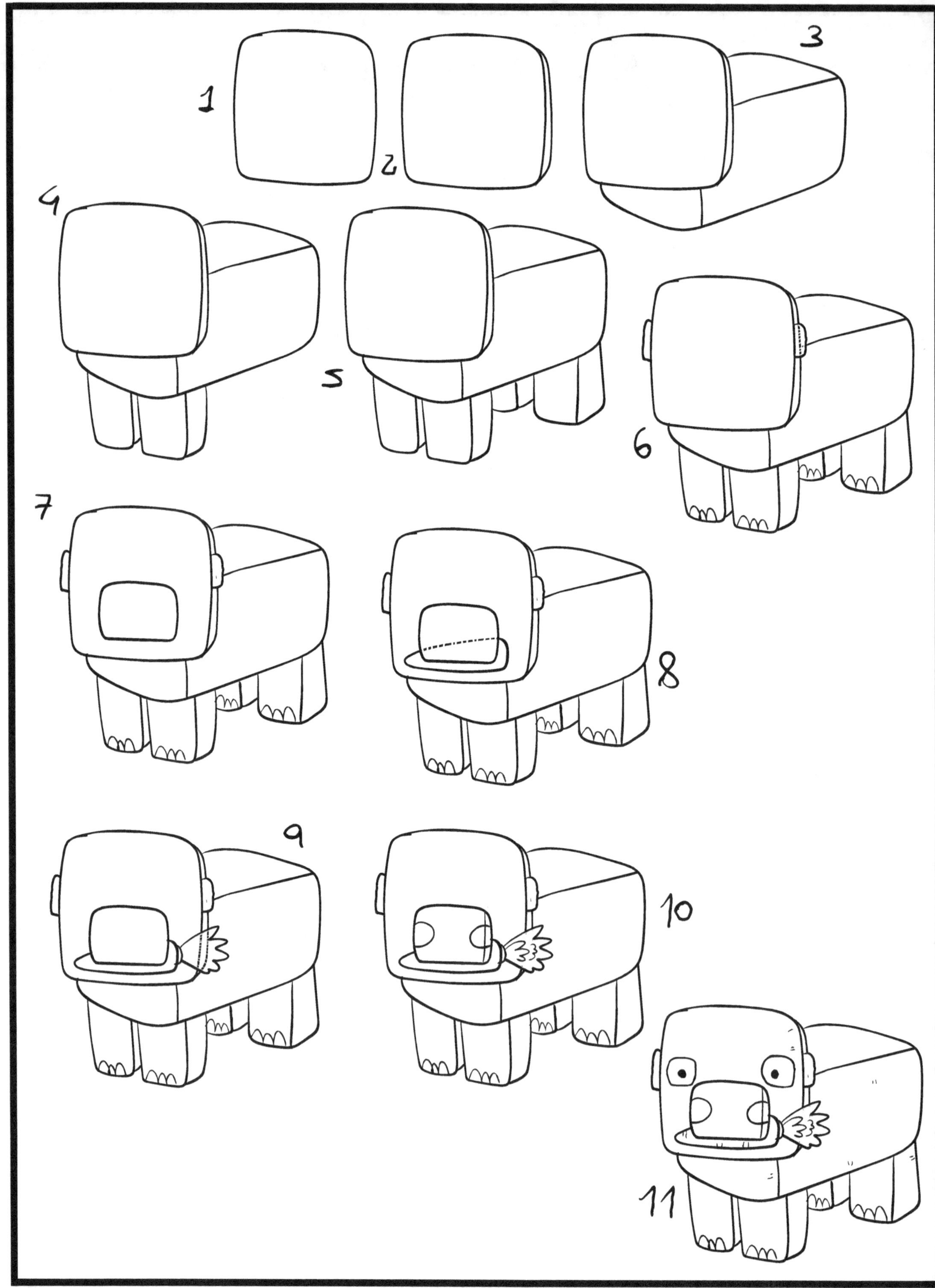

Now, it's your turn

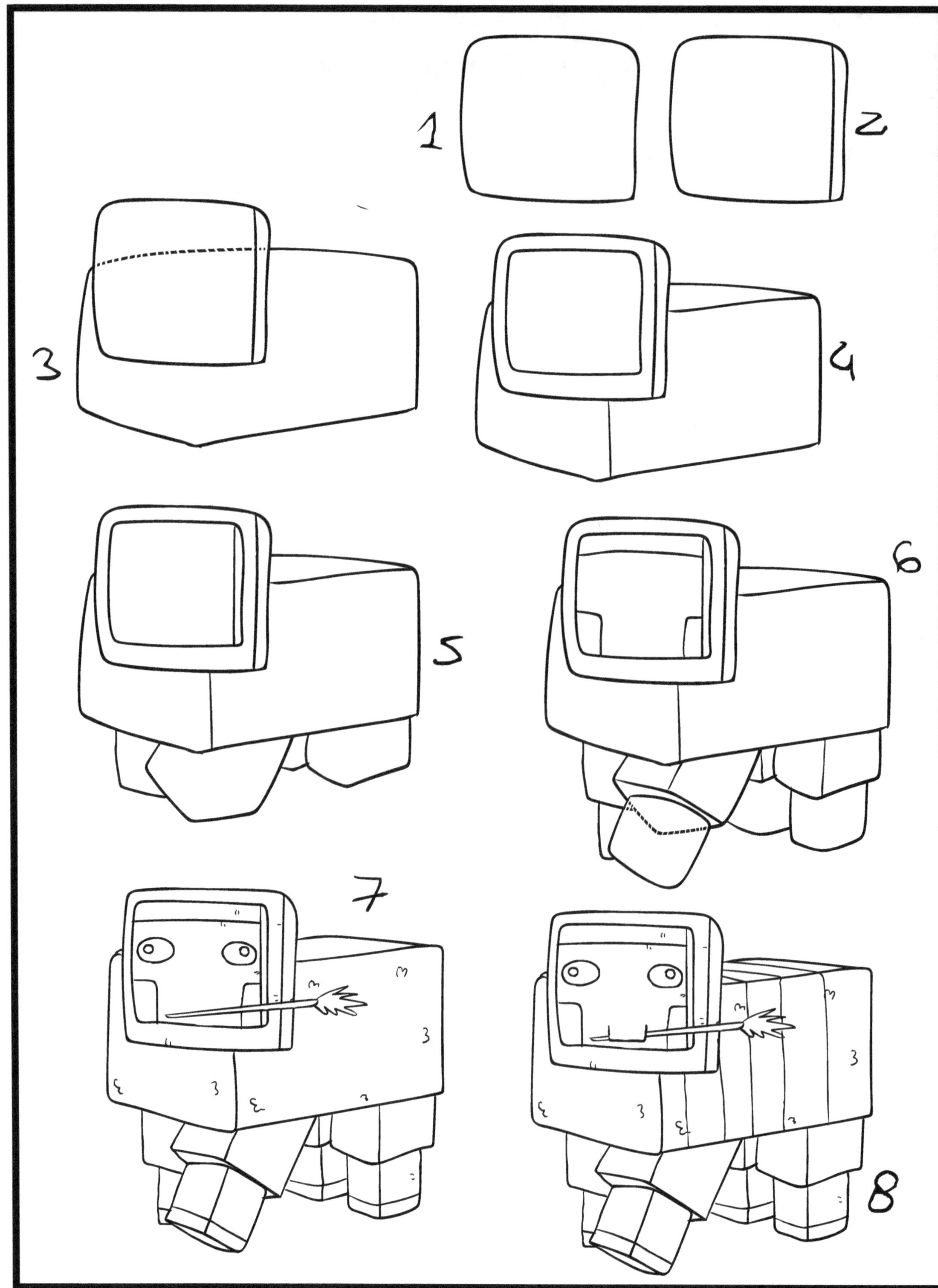
1
2
3
4
5
6
7
8

Now, it's your turn
Now, it's your turn

Now, it's your turn

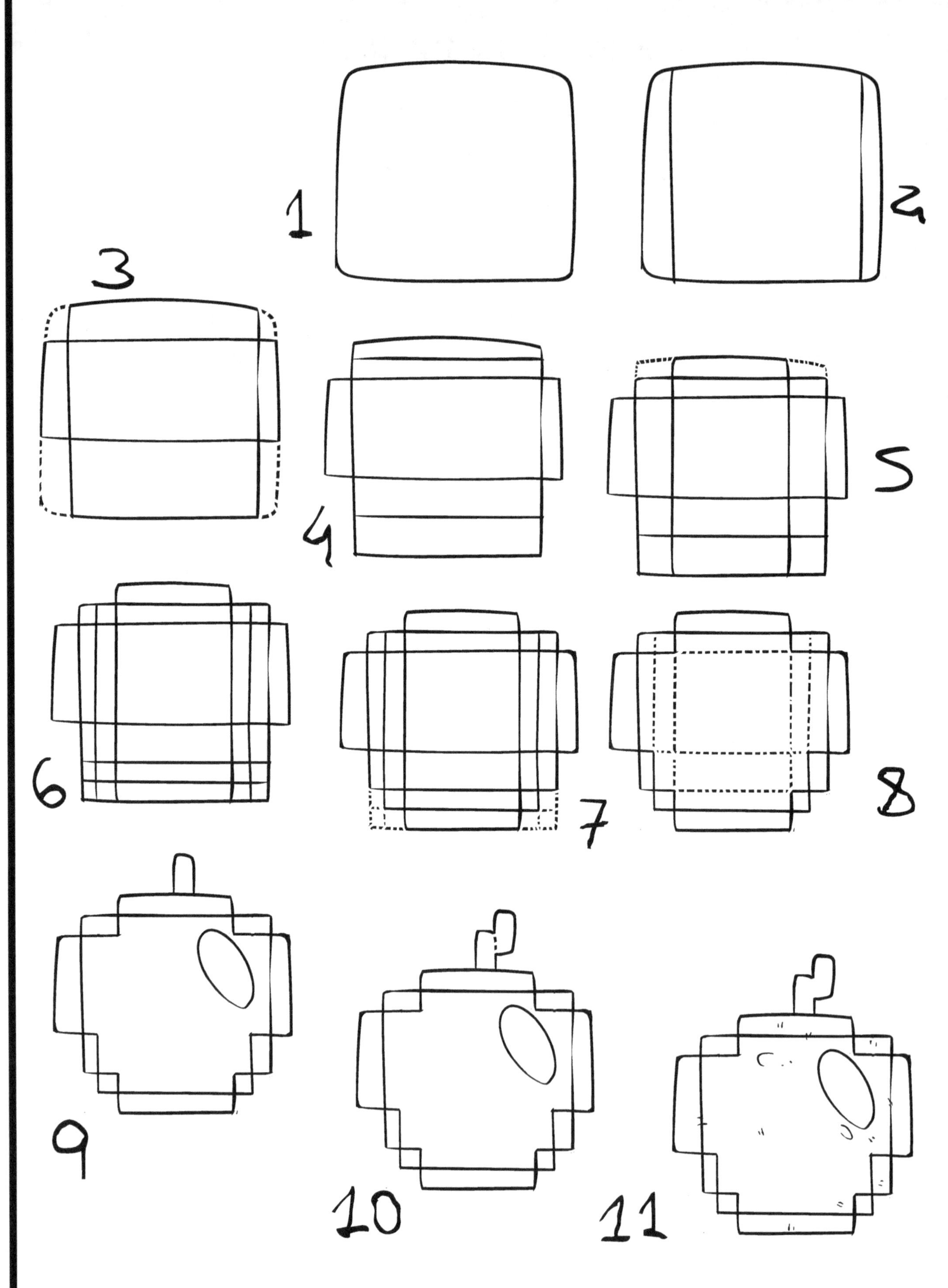

1
2
3
4
5
6
7
8
9
10
11

Now, it's your turn

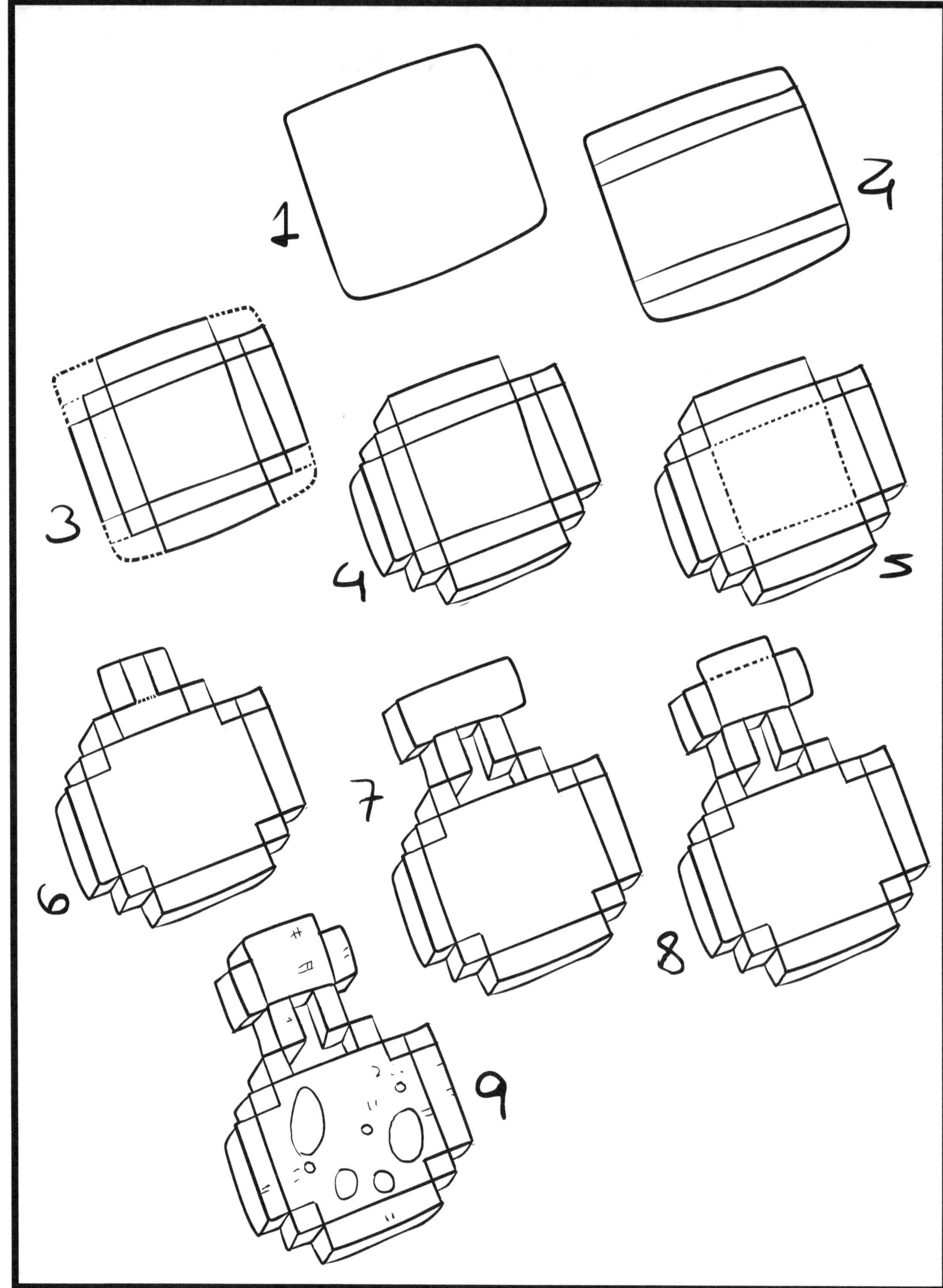

Now, it's your turn

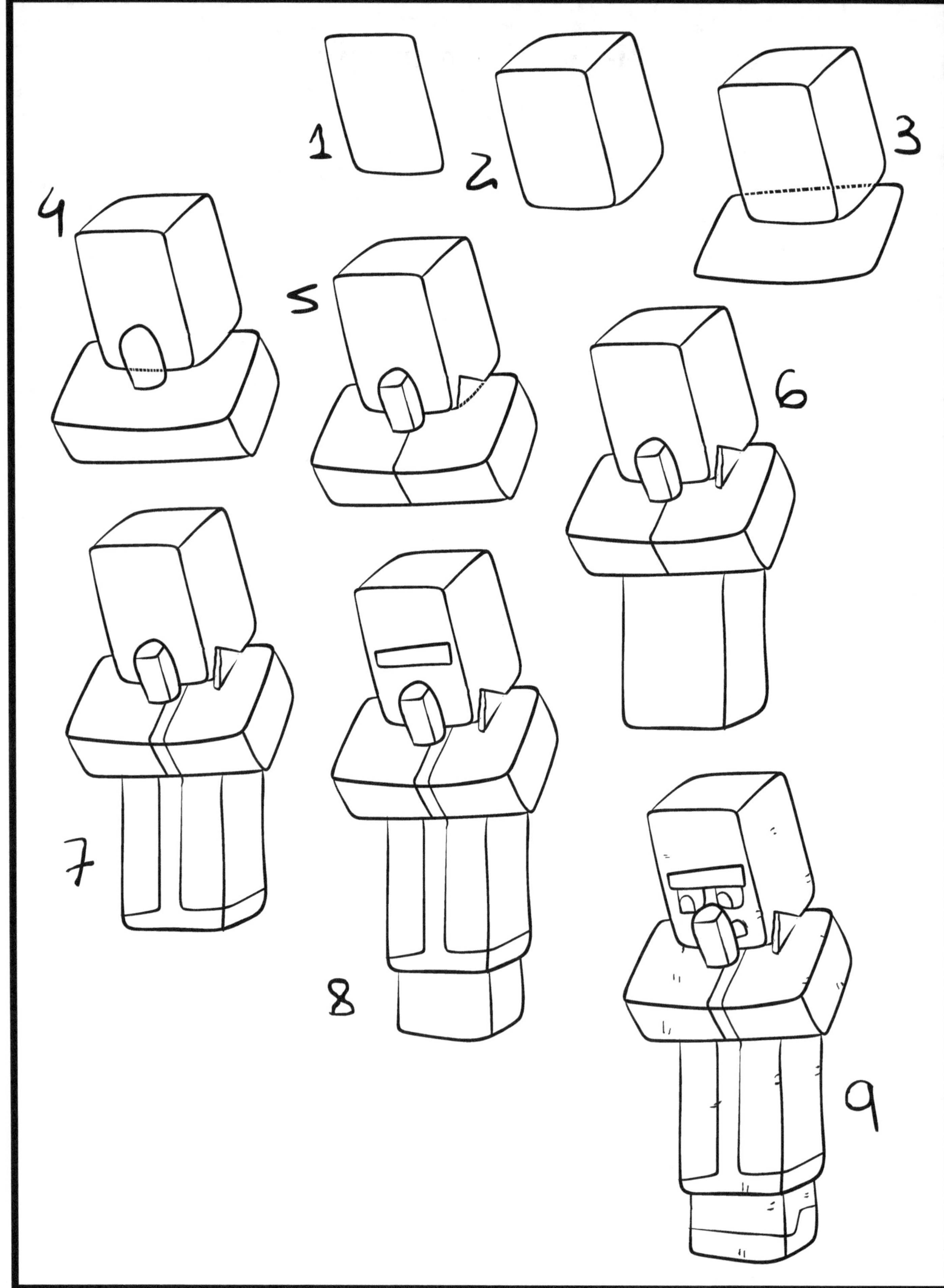

Now, it's your turn

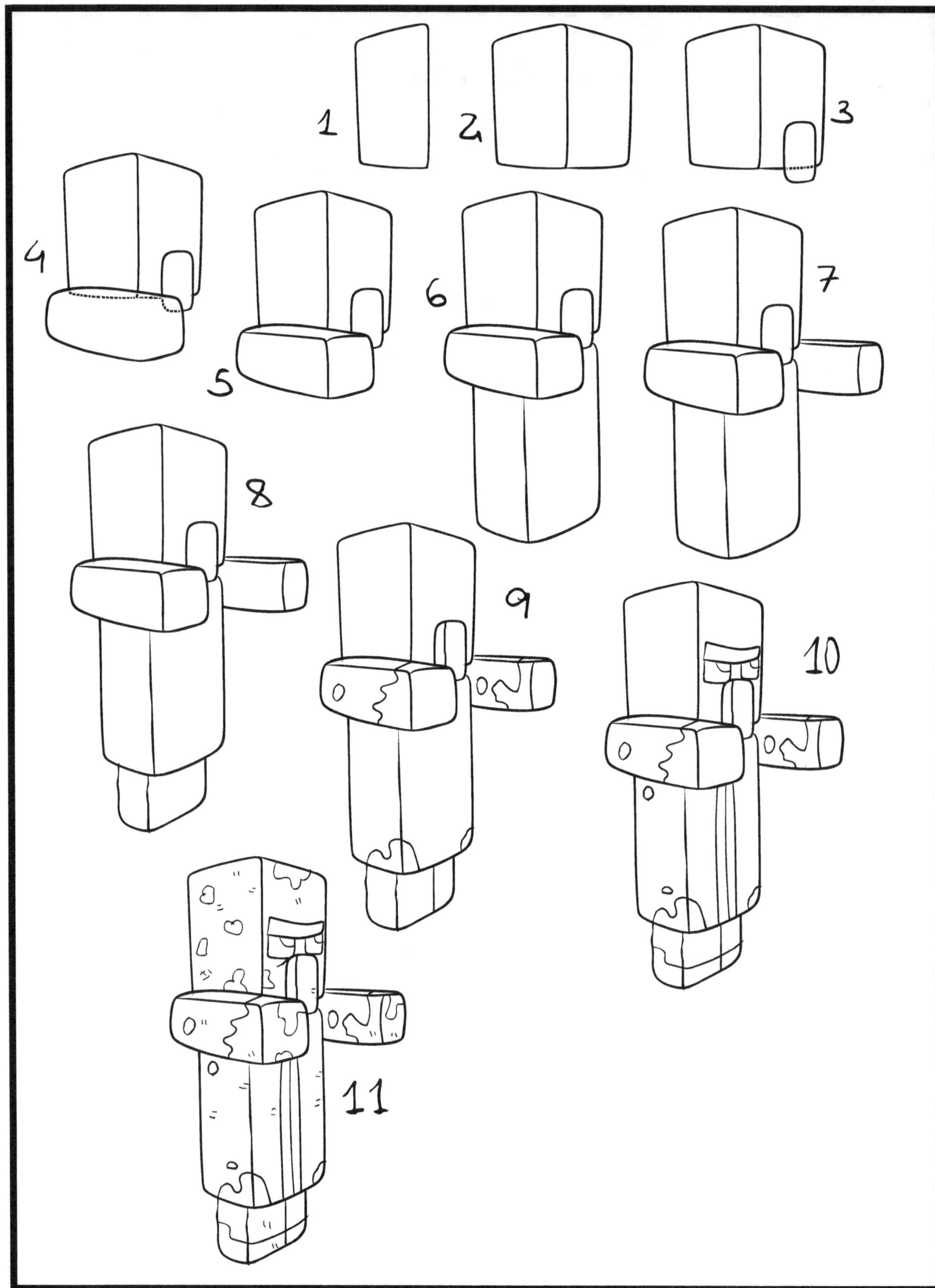

1
2
3
4
5
6
7
8
9
10
11

Now, it's your turn

Now, it's your turn

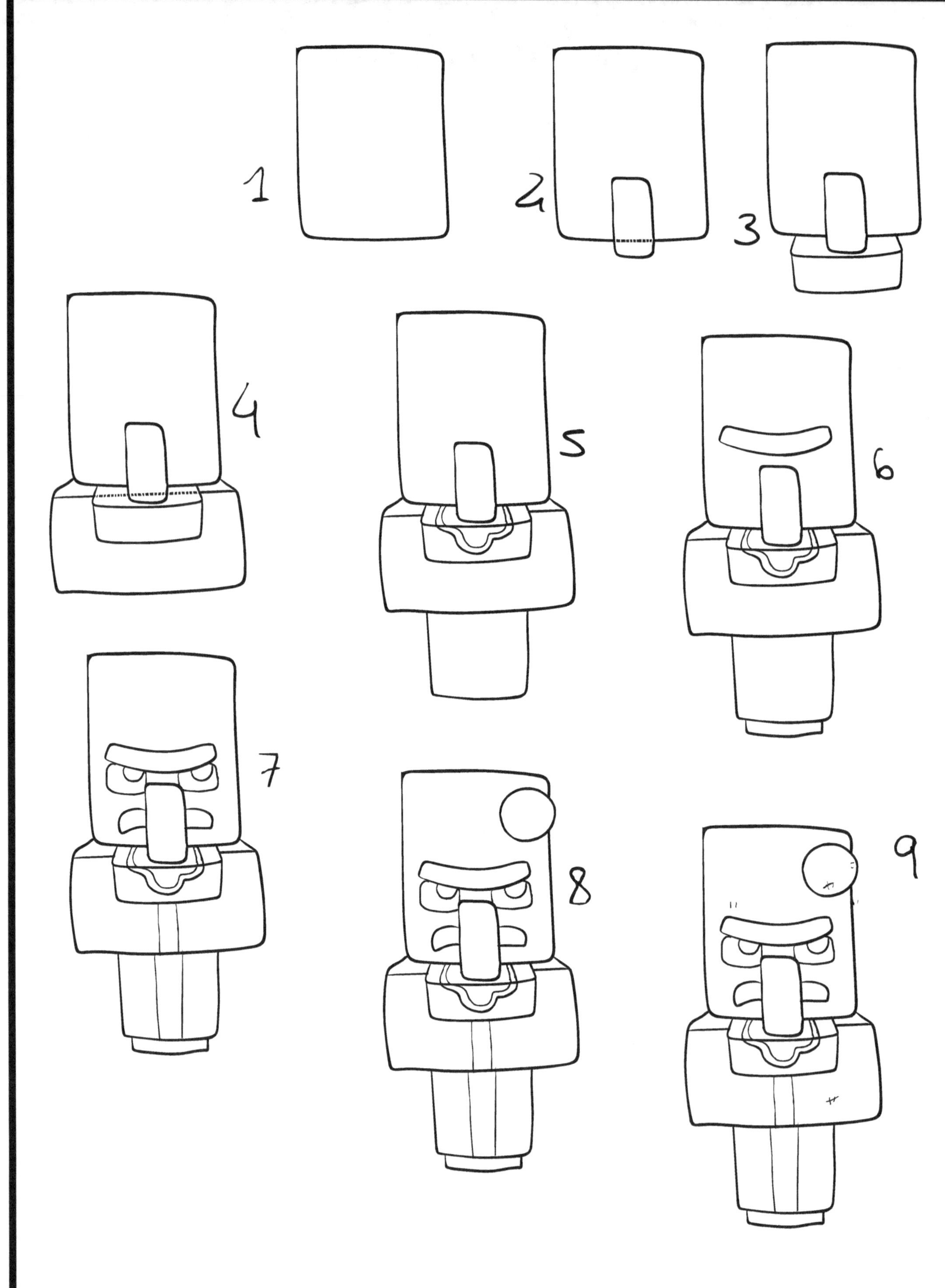

1
2
3
4
5
6
7
8
9

Now, it's your turn

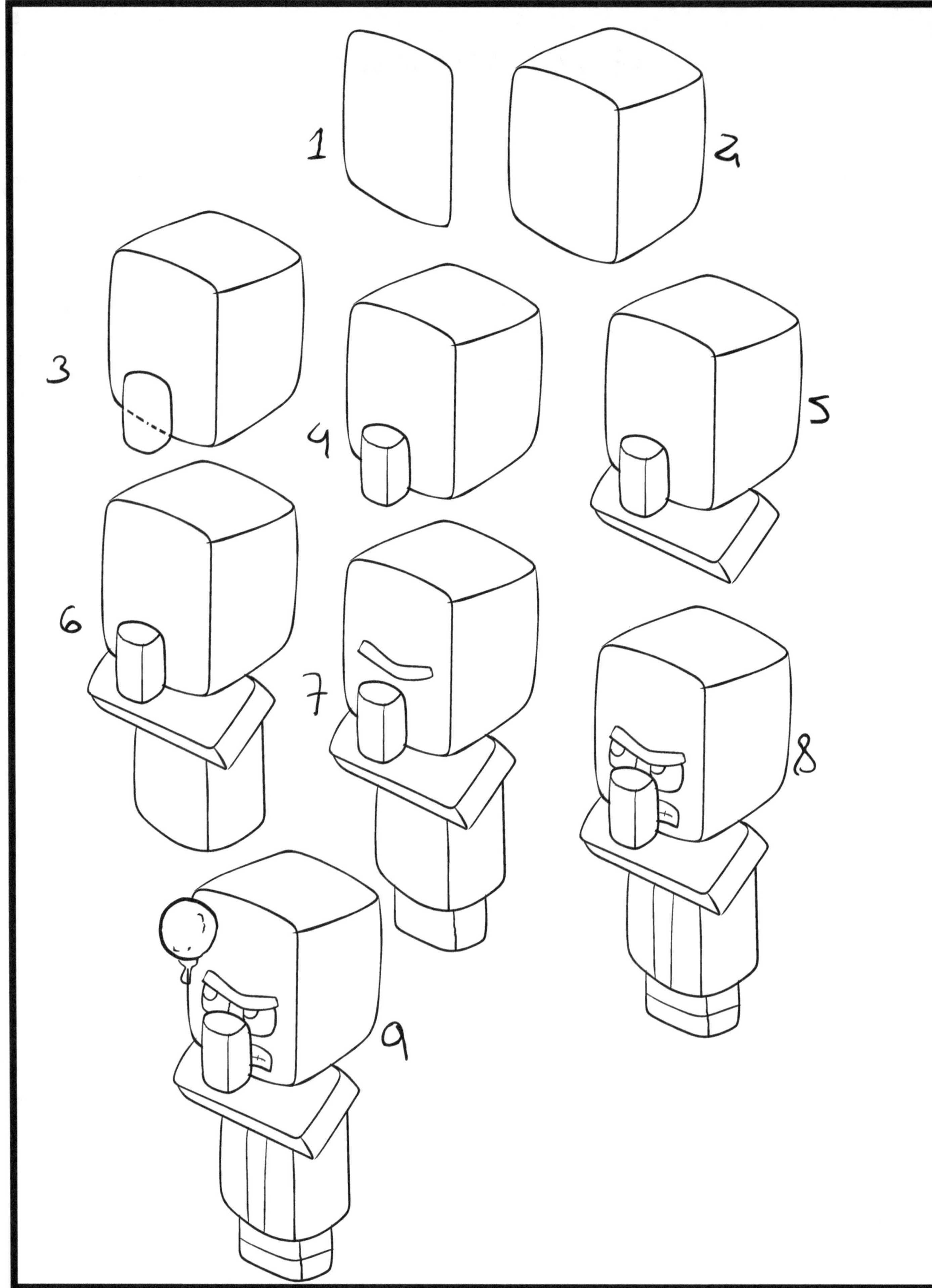

Now, it's your turn

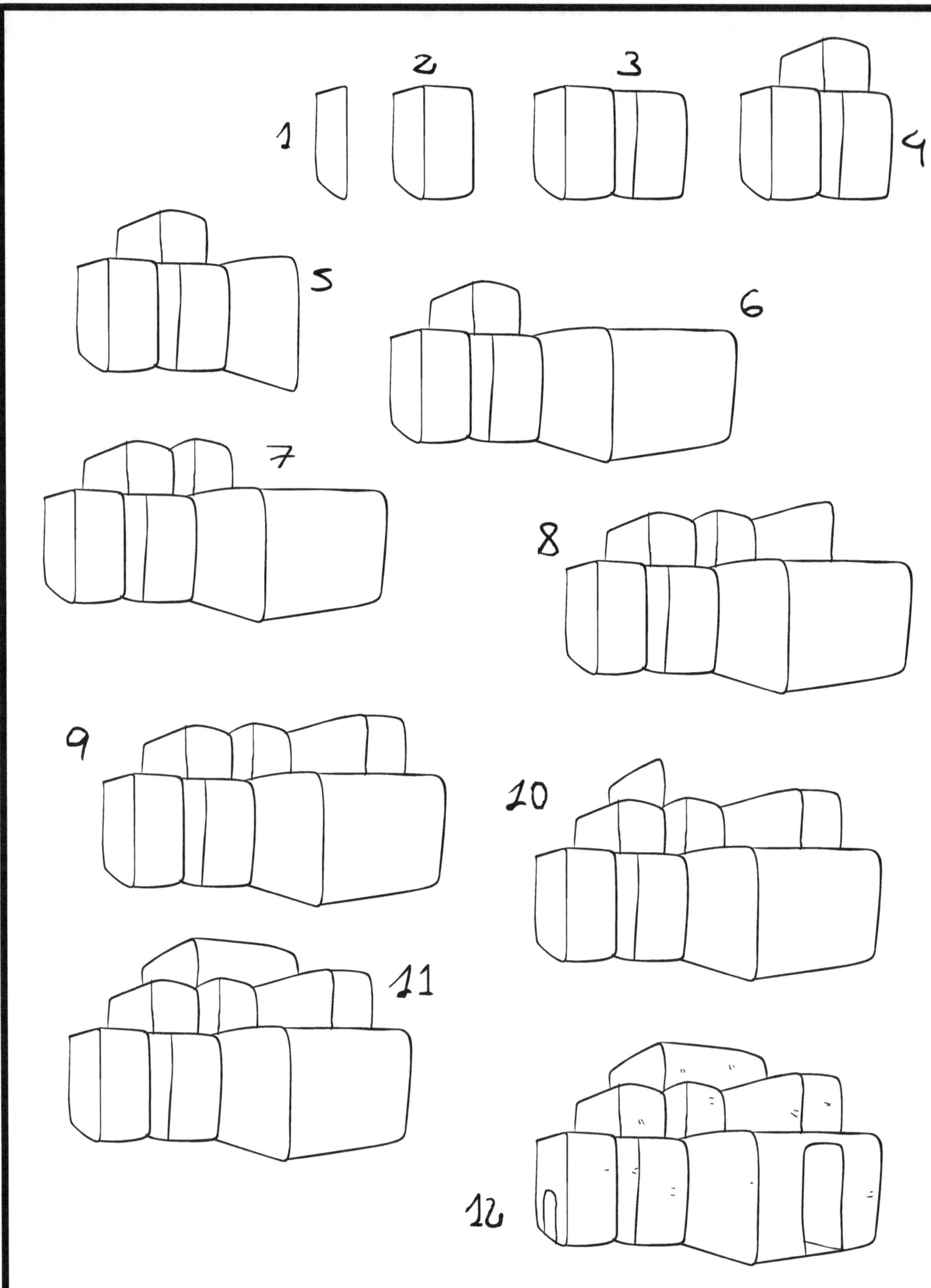

Now, it's your turn

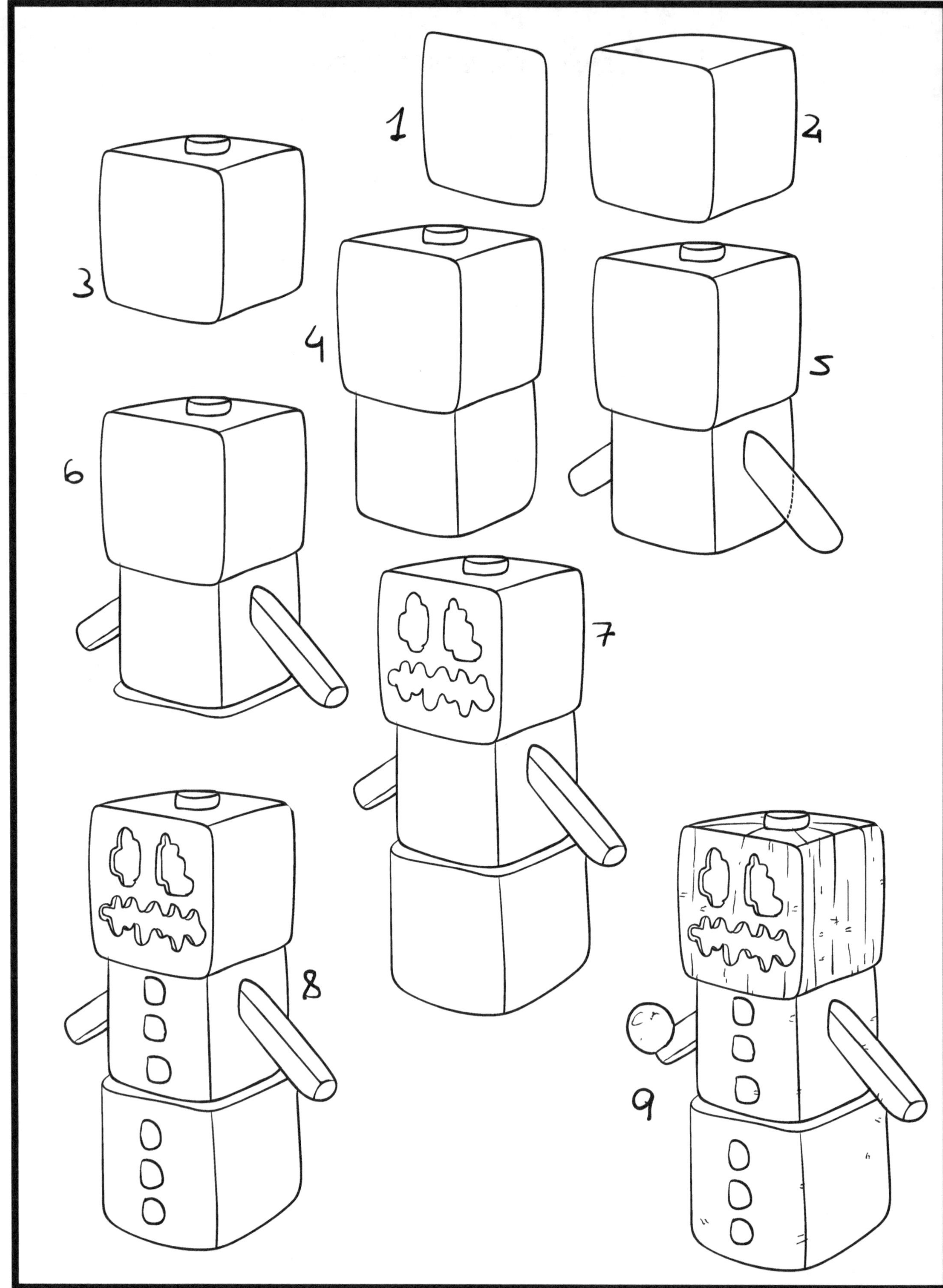

Now, it's your turn

Now, it's your turn

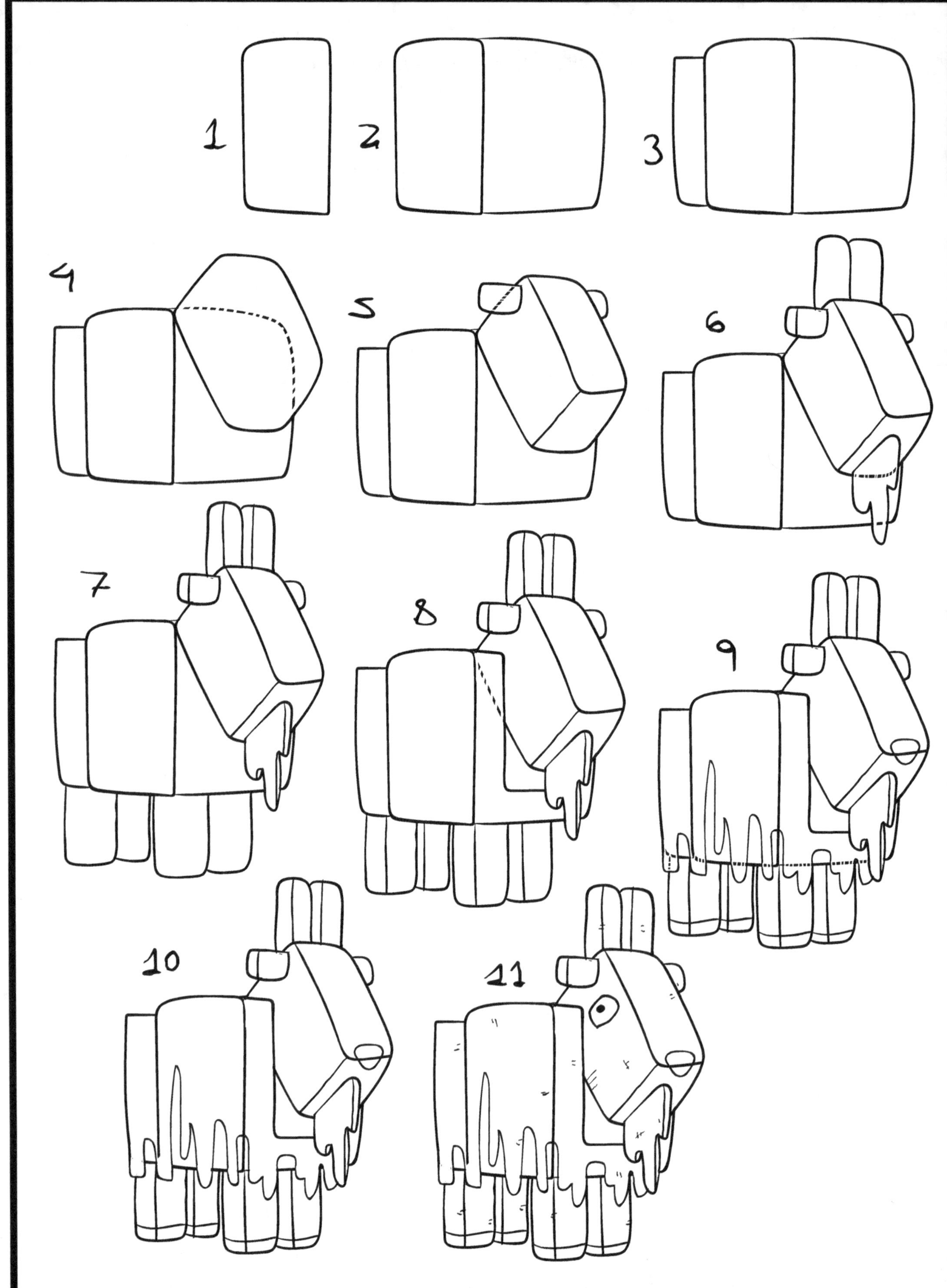
1
2
3
4
5
6
7
8
9
10
11

Now, it's your turn

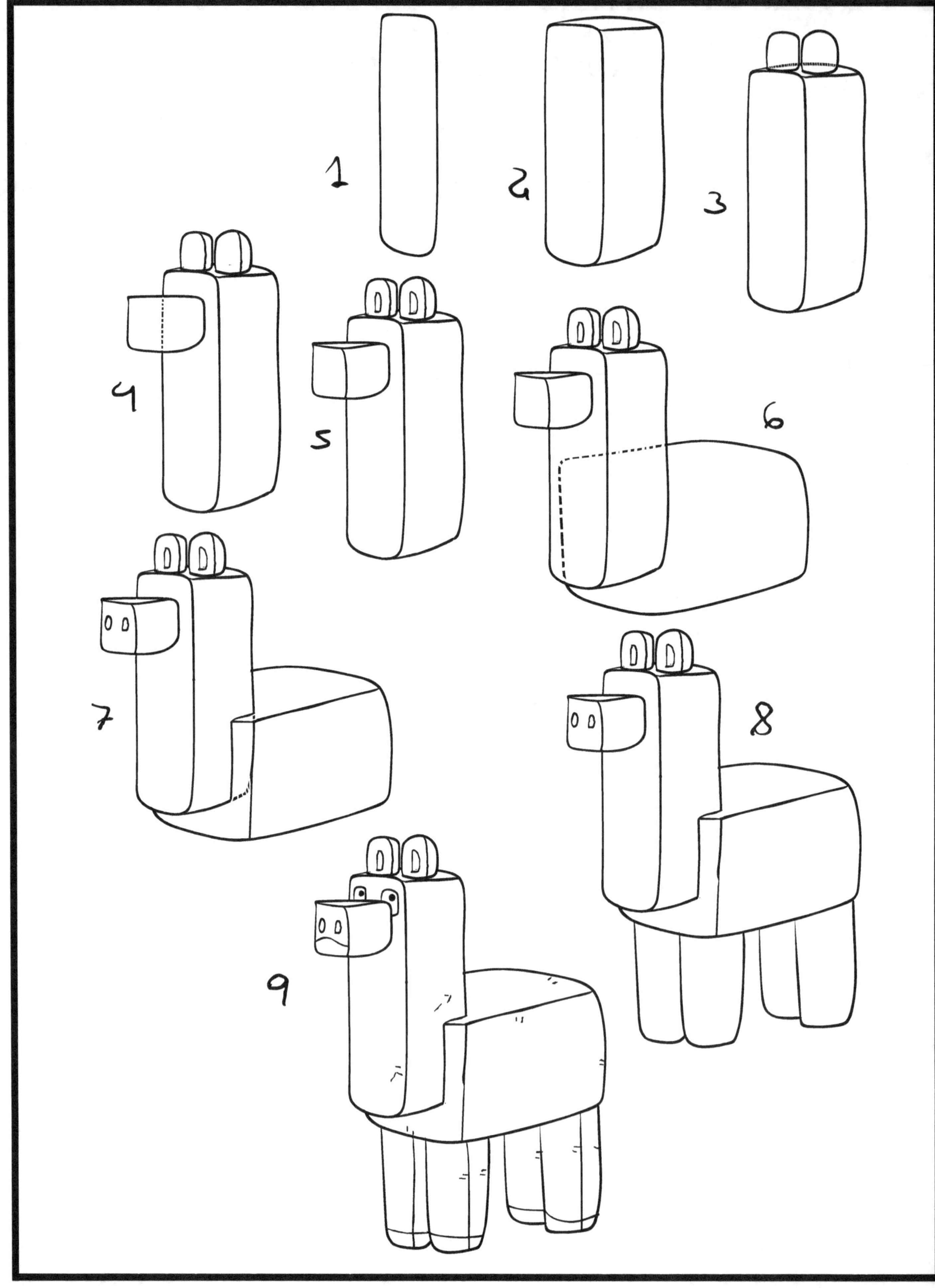

1
2
3
4
5
6
7
8
9

Now, it's your turn

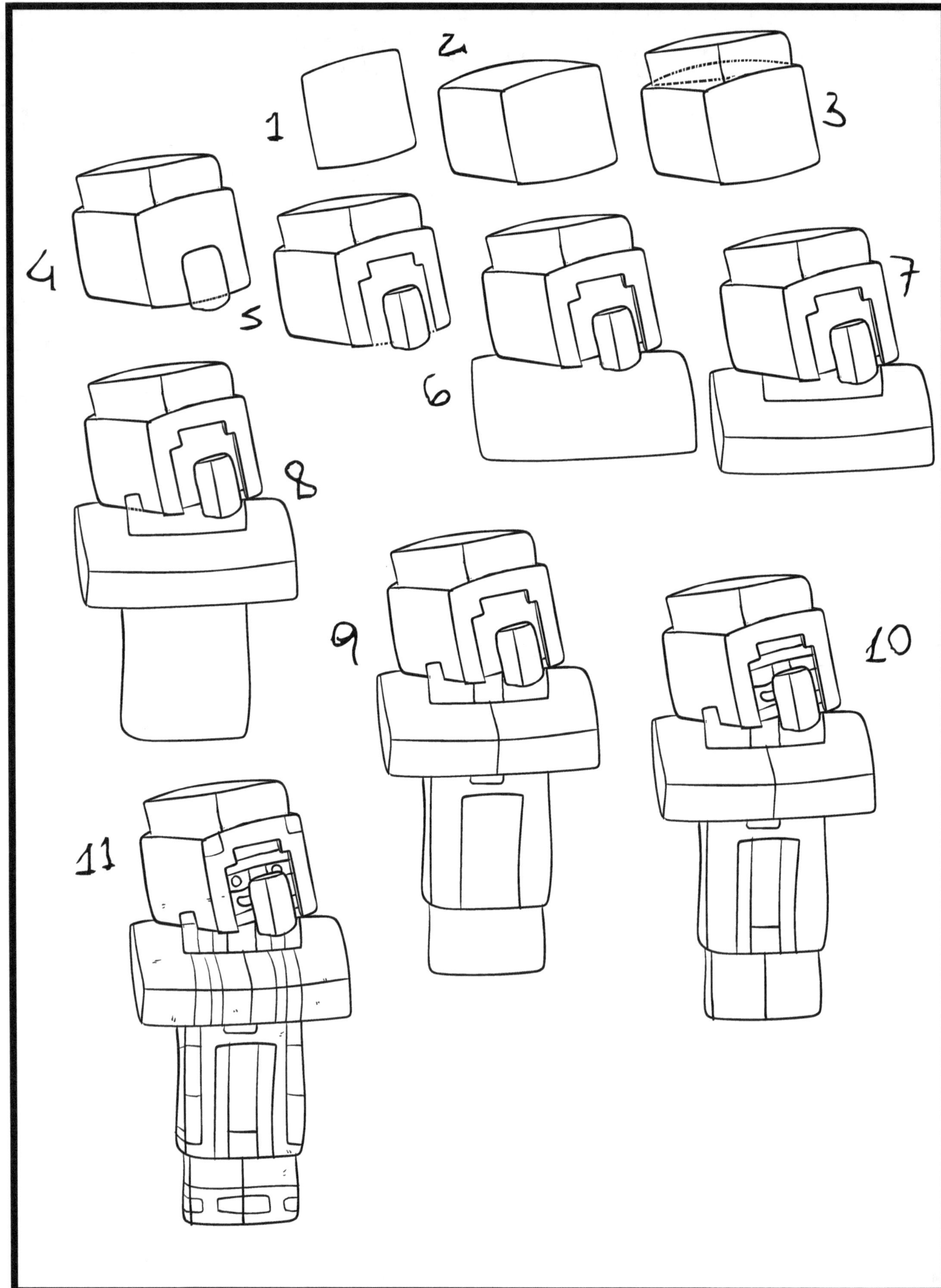

Now, it's your turn

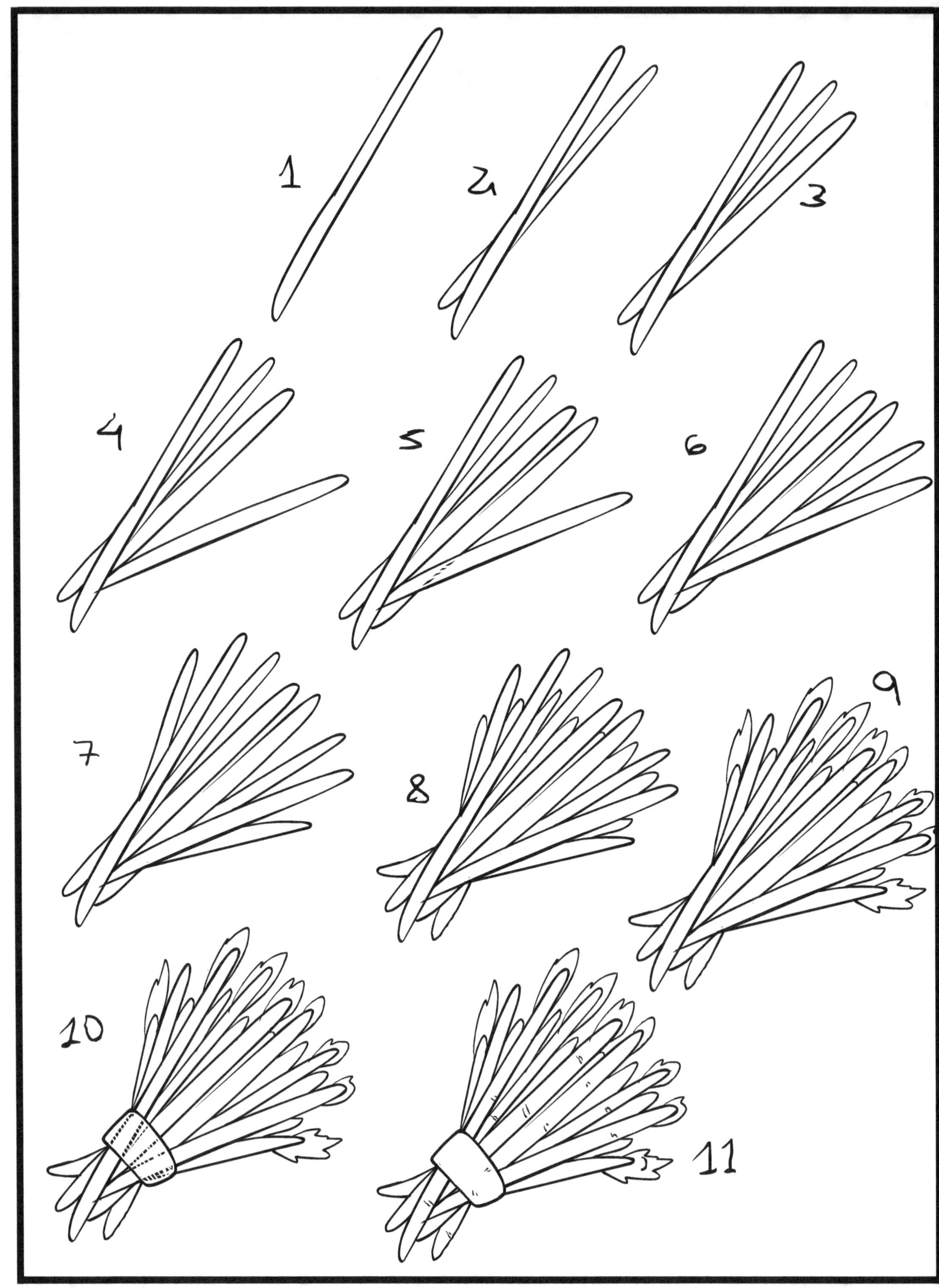

1
2
3
4
5
6
7
8
9
10
11

Now, it's your turn

Now, it's your turn

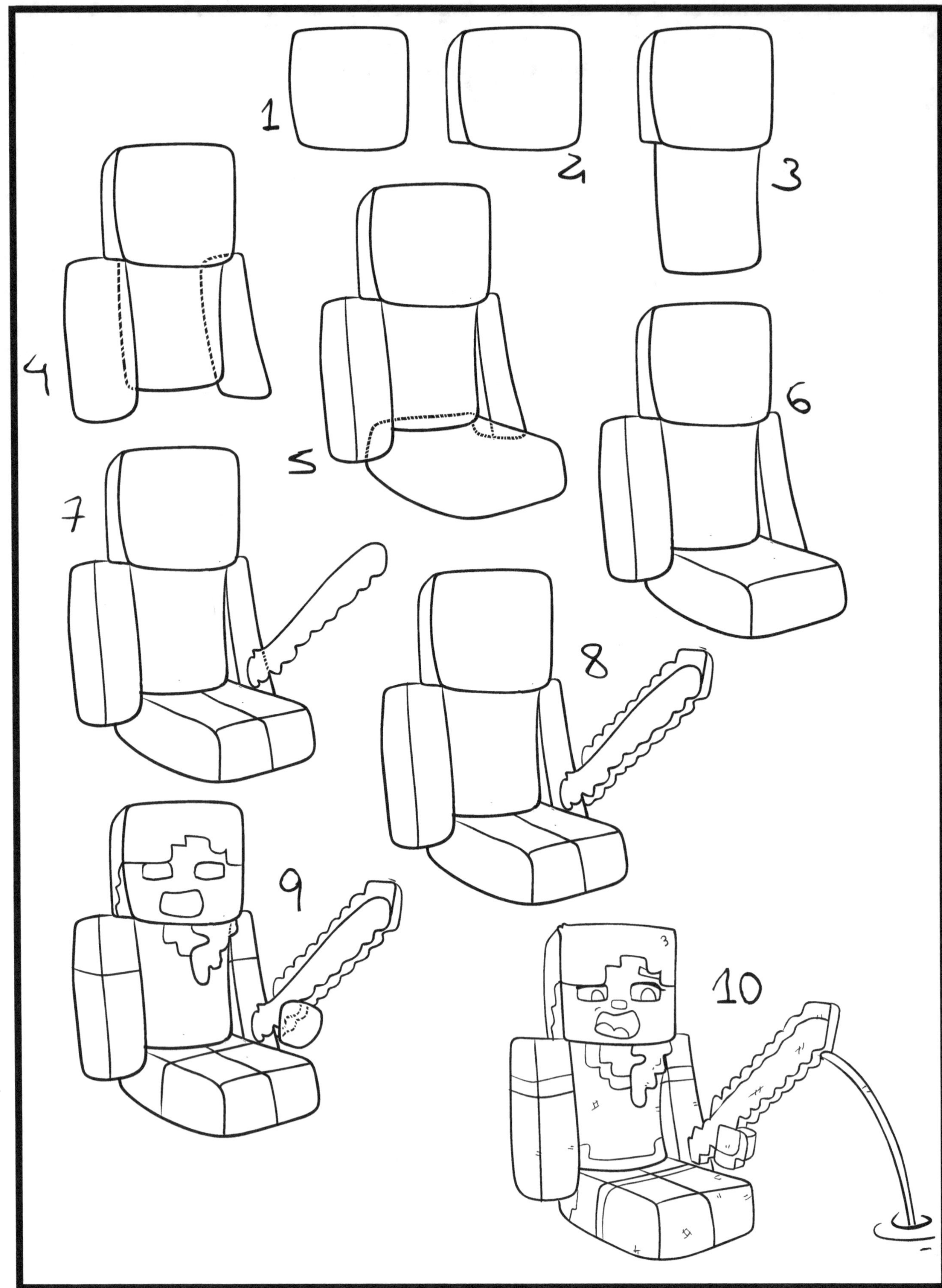

Now, it's your turn

Now, it's your turn

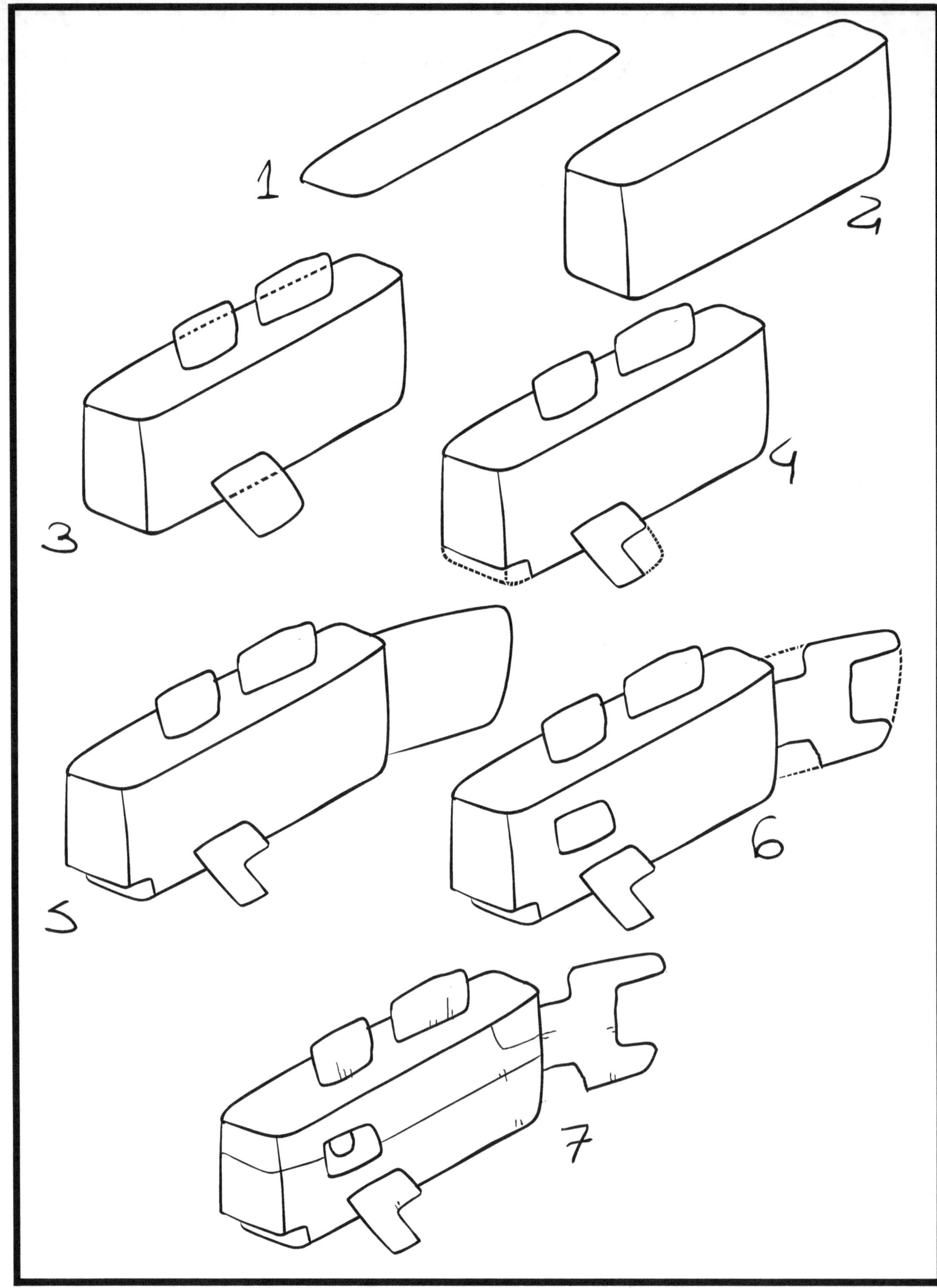

Now, it's your turn

Now, it's your turn

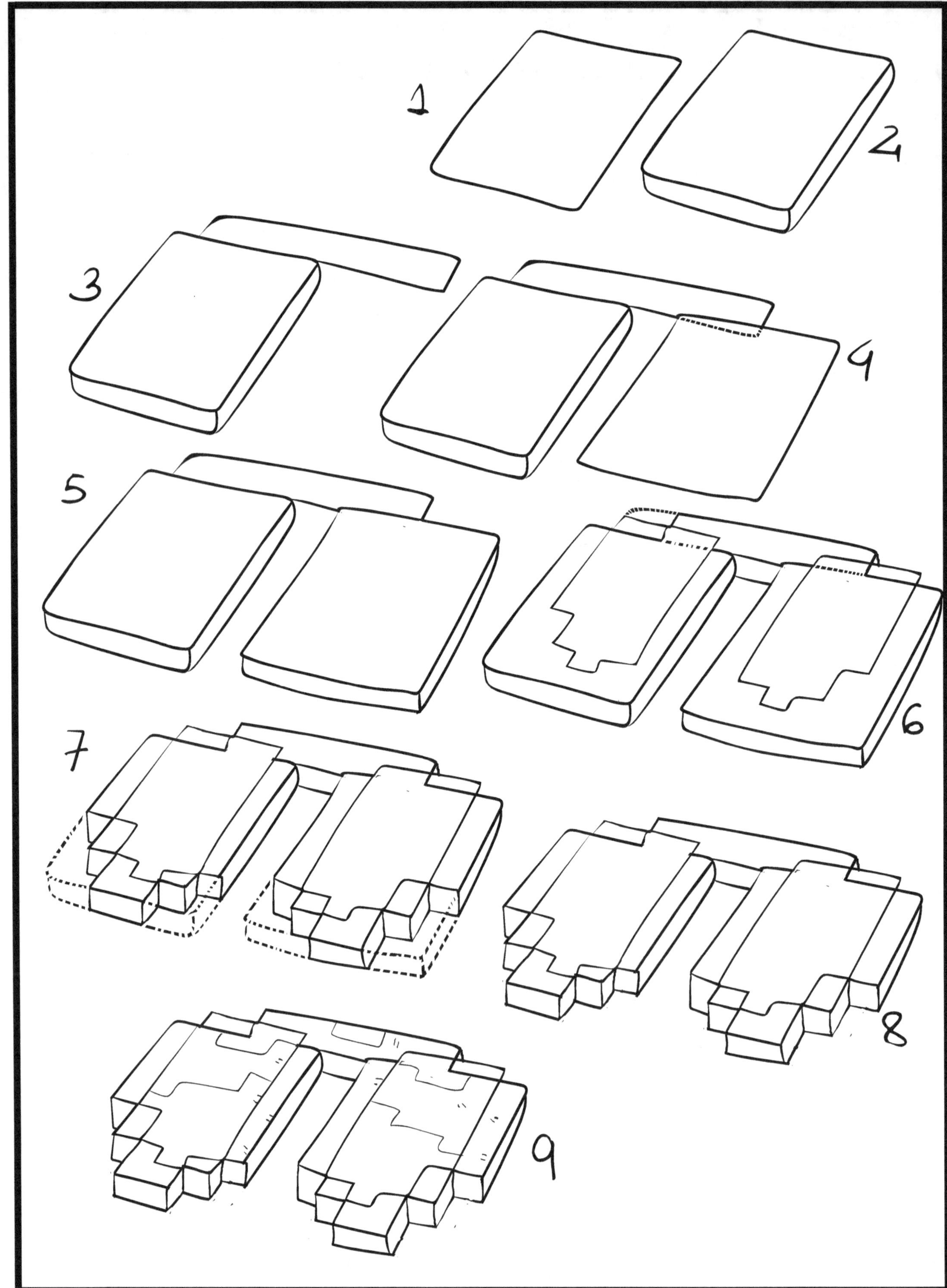

Now, it's your turn

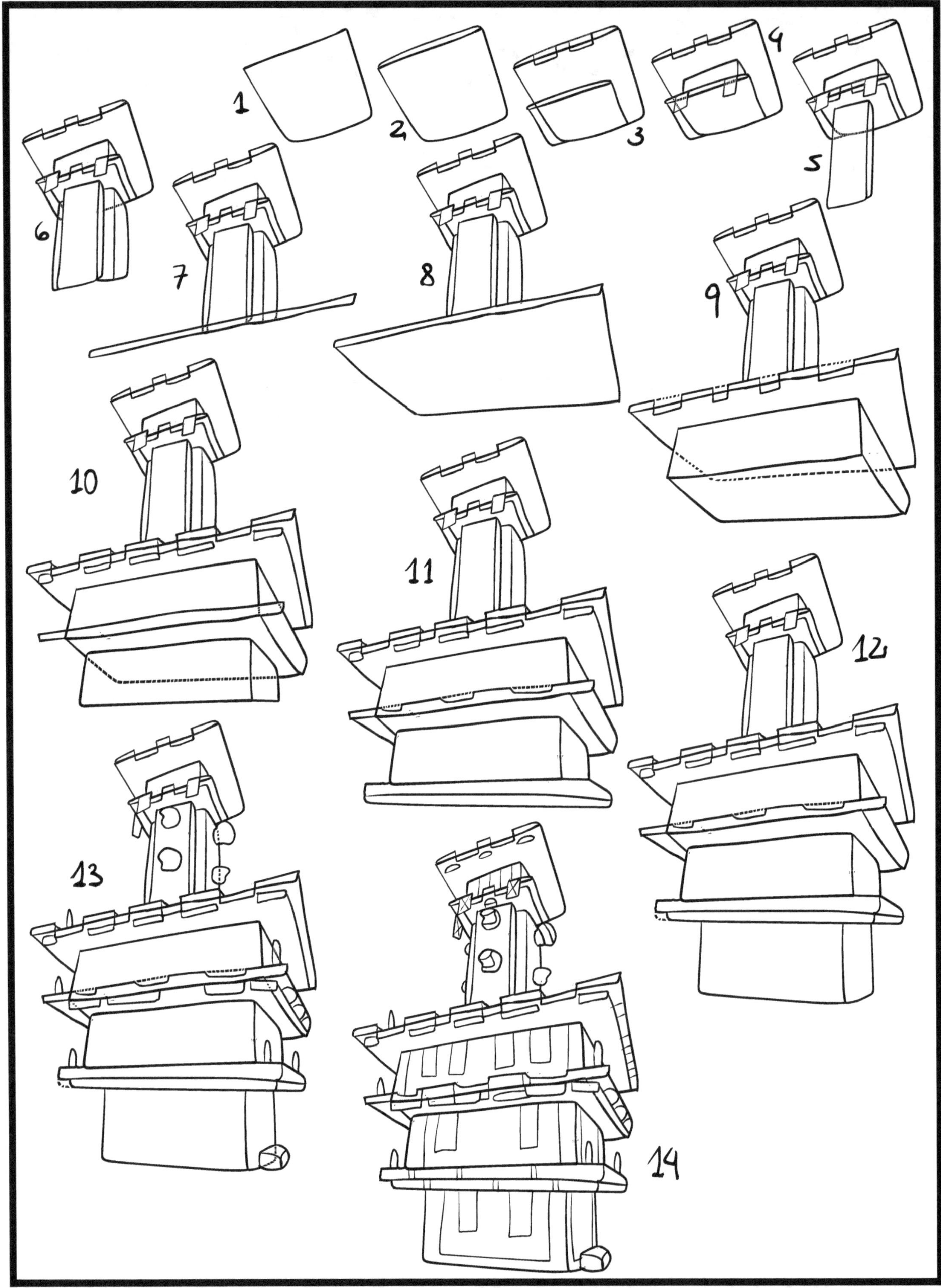

1
2
3
4
5
6
7
8
9
10
11
12
13
14

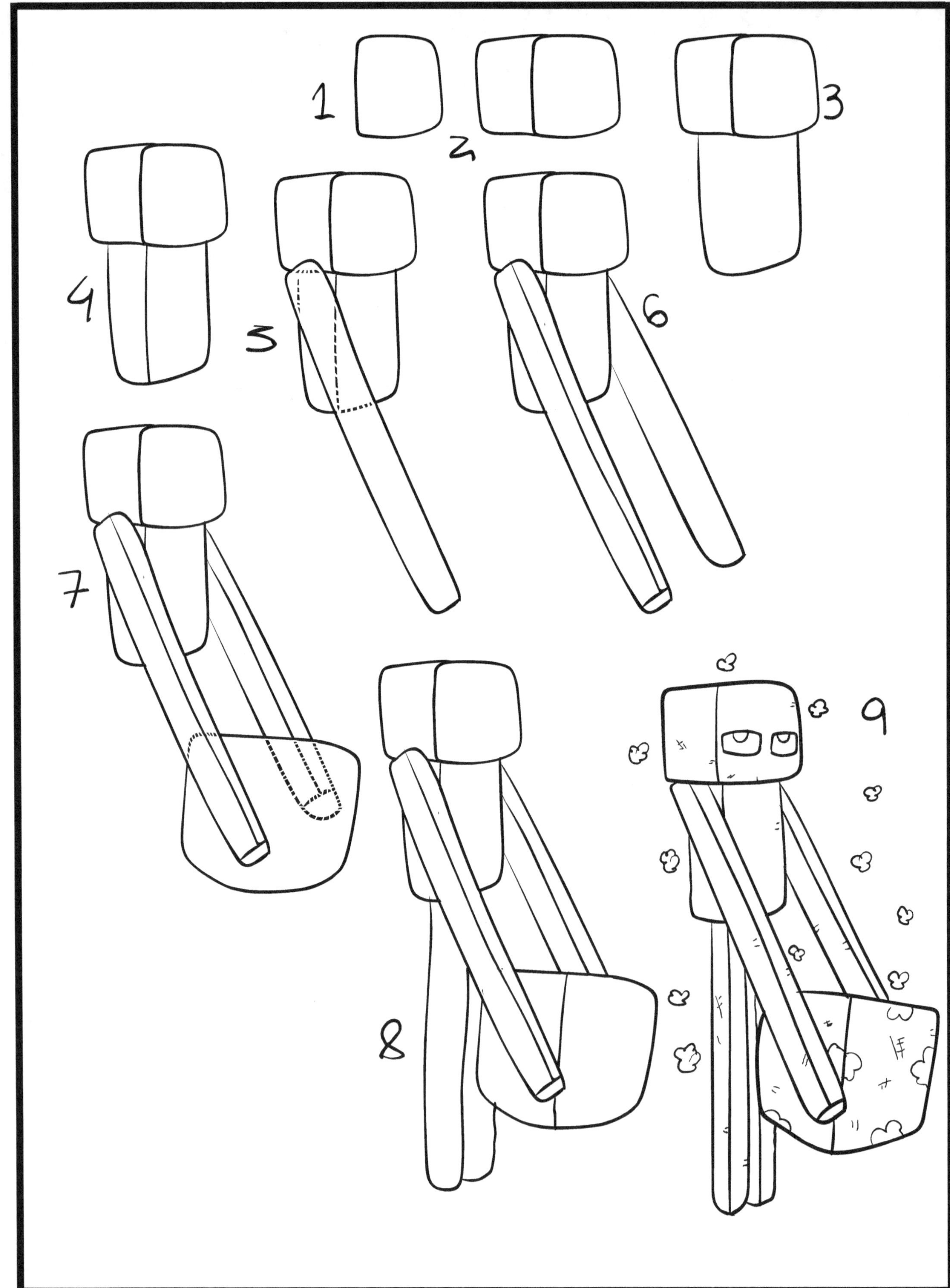

1
2
3
4
5
6
7
8
9

Now, it's your turn

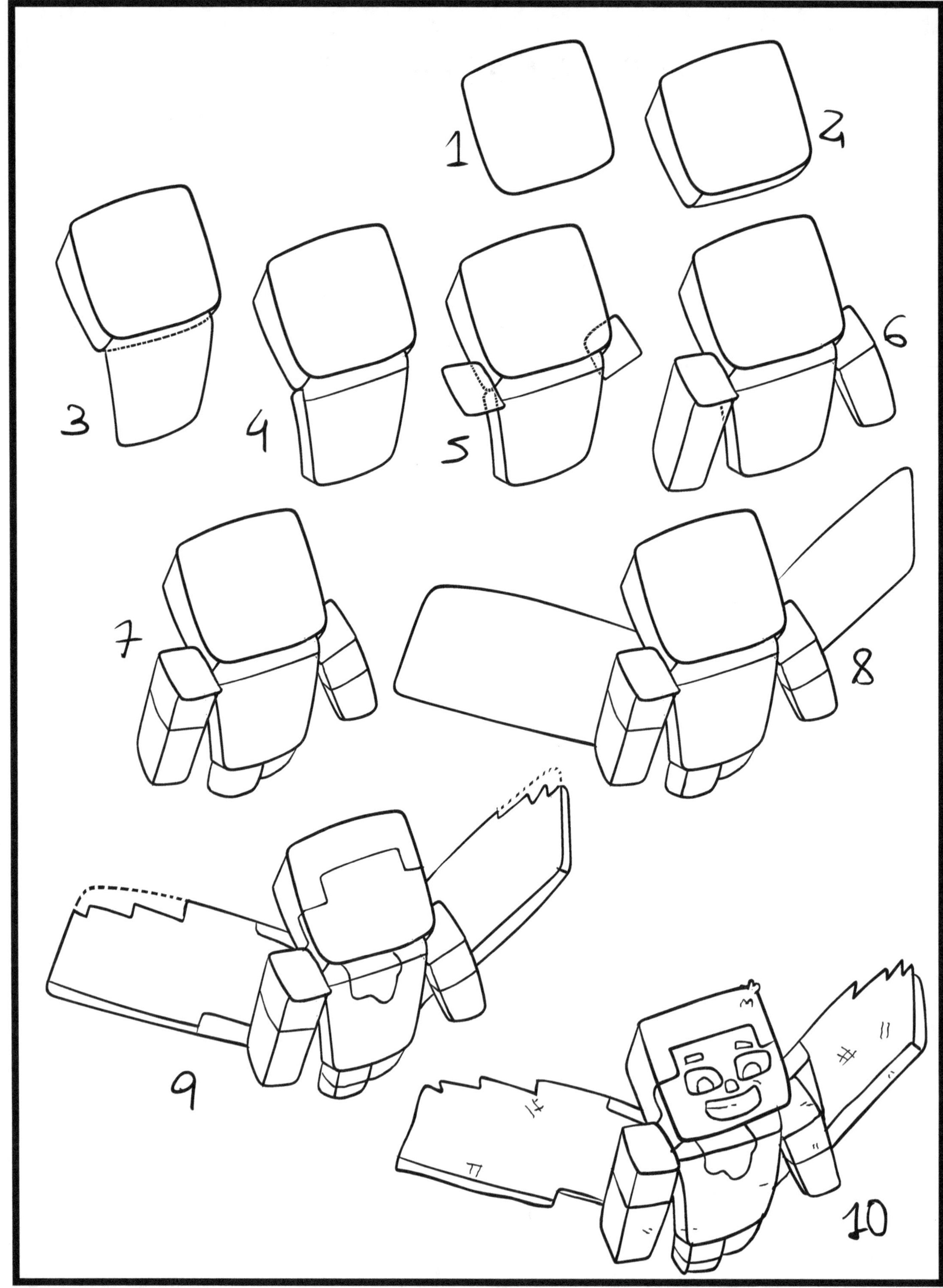
1
2
3
4
5
6
7
8
9
10

Now, it's your turn

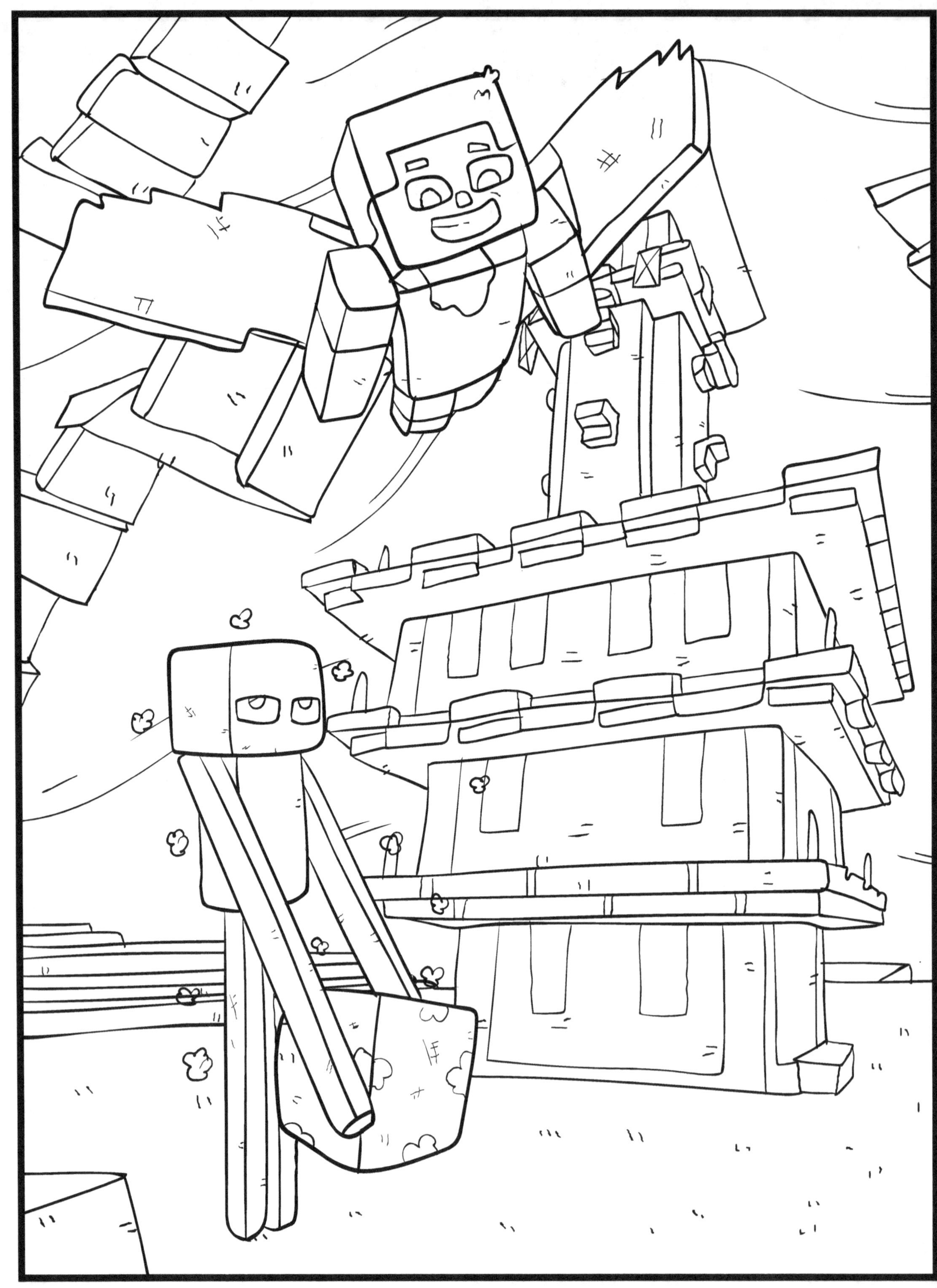

Now, it's your turn